JOHN'S EPISTLES

LIVING WITH

ASSURANCE

LifeWay Press
Nashville, TN

© 2020 LifeWay Press®

No part of this work may be reproduced or transmitted in any form or by any means, electronic or mechanical, including photocopying and recording, or by any information storage or retrieval system, except as may be expressly permitted in writing by the publisher. Requests for permission should be addressed in writing to LifeWay Press®, One LifeWay Plaza, Nashville, TN 37234.

ISBN: 978-1-5359-9257-2
Item: 005811036

Subject Area: Bible Studies
Dewey Decimal Classification Number: 227.9
Subject Heading: New Testament Epistles
Printed in the United States of America

LifeWay Christian Resources
One LifeWay Plaza
Nashville, TN 37234

CONTENTS

JOHN'S EPISTLES: LIVING WITH ASSURANCE

I am a glutton for punishment. As a full-time pastor with a wife and four kids at home, I decided to embark on a Ph.D. I have always loved learning, especially about things I can use to sharpen my ministry skills. As I progressed through the degree program, I found the work to be rewarding and encouraging. That was true until I enrolled in the course entitled "Inferential Statistics." I have never been a math guy, so this course required me to put in many extra hours of practice. The hardest part of the course was not learning the formulas and how to work them but reading the problem and choosing the right formula to solve the problem correctly. It did not matter if I put all the numbers into the equation correctly if I chose the wrong formula to use. This is much the same in our spiritual lives. When we face difficult situations in life, it is vital we understand rightly the things of God. His truth is the only way to see clearly through the fog of life. If we misunderstand or misappropriate a spiritual doctrine, it can devastate our faith, our walk with Jesus, or perhaps even our eternity.

It is from that setting that the apostle John wrote his letters. John wrote to instruct believers about a correct understanding of who Jesus is and why right doctrine really matters. He desired for them to see how their understanding of who Jesus is had real impact on their daily lives, decisions, and future. To see this in context, we know John wrote these letters as a response to disagreement among believers about correct theology and conduct. In his earlier Gospel (John 14:6-7), John recorded these words from Jesus: "I am the way, the truth, and the life. No one comes to the Father except through me. If you know me, you will also know my Father." John may have had these words on his mind as he wrote these three letters. He knew his readers needed to see the truth about who Jesus is, and

Sea of Galilee from Hippos. John was called to follow Jesus from his fishing profession in Galilee (Luke 5:9-11).

ILLUSTRATOR PHOTO/ BRENT BRUCE (60/9593)

he was concerned false teaching about Jesus had risen among the people, primarily that He had not been raised bodily from the grave.

John also had another concern. When we do not rightly understand the gospel, then we do not rightly understand sin. A robust teaching on the nature and mission of Jesus leads us to a right understanding of our sin. When false doctrine creeps in, the effect usually minimizes the destructive nature of our sin. We fail to see how sin impacts our thinking and living. This is a dangerous place to live. The Scripture often reminds us of the dangers involved in sinful living (Gal. 5:19-21; Col. 3:5-6; Jas. 1:15). John encouraged his readers (and us today) to have right thinking on the doctrine of the gospel in order to protect ourselves from the dangers of living in sin.

Lastly, John brought a word of encouragement to his audience. He reminded them continually of the great love God had for them. Therefore, they should love others. Love is the centerpiece of the gospel; it ought to be the centerpiece of a Christ-follower's life. When we walk in this love for Jesus, and toward others, we can be assured we have eternal life in Jesus. Our salvation never comes through our works (only by faith in Christ), but someone who demonstrates no love for Jesus nor for others most certainly does not posses a saving faith.

The Letters of John should serve as a blueprint for us as we examine our doctrine in light of the gospel of the Lord Jesus. They should help us to live under the truth that sin is deadly and should be taken seriously. They should also help us to see the love of God and our love for others are key to walking faithfully in the kingdom.

It is possible 1 John was meant to be a cover letter for the Gospel of John. The gnostic heresy of the first century forms the background for both books. The Gospel has an evangelistic thrust, while 1 John is written to believers.

Date, Setting, and Author

Before we examine in great detail the teachings of these letters, it is vital to understand their context and audience. Most conservative scholars agree the three letters where written by the apostle John (author of the Fourth Gospel). This consensus is not only a modern understanding, but dates back to early church leaders such as Irenaeus, Dionysius of Alexandria, and Tertullian. The apostle John, also known as the disciple Jesus loved (John 21:20,24), was called to follow Jesus from the fishing profession in Galilee (Luke 5:9-11). He, along with his brother James, were sometimes called the "Sons of Thunder" (Mark 3:17).

The first two of John's Letters appear to be written to churches in Asia Minor (modern-day Turkey). Ephesus was the largest and most prominent city in the region. It was known to be both beautiful and wealthy. Ephesus was the leading trade center of the Roman Empire in the region. It was a cosmopolitan city full of pagan worship. The temple of Artemis (Diana) was located there. This temple was considered one of the Seven Wonders of the Ancient World.

From Ephesus it is likely these letters were passed throughout the churches in the region in order to teach and encourage believers. The third letter has a more personal nature. It is addressed to a man name Gaius, who appears to have been a personal friend of John's. In this letter John praised Gaius for his faithfulness and his hospitality to fellow believers as they shared the gospel during missionary travels.

There is some debate as to when these letters were written. As previously noted, some even argue that 1 John is a cover letter to John's Gospel. However, most scholars date these letters late in the first century, between AD 85-95. This would allow enough time after the life and ministry of Jesus

Modern fish nets on the dock at Kavalla (biblical Neapolis).

for issues such as Gnosticism (false teaching that believed the spirit was good but the flesh was bad) and Docetism (form of Gnosticism that taught Jesus was not really human, but only took on the appearance of a physical body). These are two of the primary heresies that John wrote to correct.

Focus for Us

John wrote these letters to address issues in the church of Asia Minor during the first century; however, the issues he addressed have significant relevance for how believers in Christ should worship and live today. As noted earlier, John wrote to correct false teaching and doctrine as well as to encourage believers to love God and others through both word and deed. While the conversations we have with those in our communities might not be directly related to the incarnation of Jesus or the philosophical understanding of humanity, we are having complex conversations with our neighbors. The topics of marriage, sexuality, gender, science, and ethics are in the news every day. We wrestle with how we love people who see the world differently because of their political views, their cultures, or their backgrounds. It is vital to our witness as Christ-followers that we are able to converse with others in our spheres of influence in ways that reflects both the light of the gospel but also the love of the gospel.

Organization

To organize our study, we will divide 1 John into five sessions, then spend one session each on 2 John and 3 John. Here is a breakdown and theme for each of our sessions.

1. Fellowship with God (1 John 1:1–2:2)
In these verses we will examine what our relationship with God looks like. We will see how sin has destroyed us, but that through our confession of sin and turning to faith in Christ we can experience new life. This new life is a source of great joy!

2. Remaining with God (1 John 2:3-27)
In this section we will see how John used the themes of light and darkness to help us examine our motives and actions. John admonished and encouraged believers in their walk with God.

3. Living as God's Children (1 John 2:28–3:10; 4:1-6)
Those who are God's children hate sin and desire to walk in the righteousness

that comes from a relationship with Jesus. God's Spirit marks those who are His true children.

4. Living with Love (1 John 3:11-24; 4:7-21)

We will find the importance of love in the life of a believer. Love is the true measuring stick of one's relationship with God. Do we love Him or do we love the world? John said those who love Him are truly His children.

5. Living as Conquerors (1 John 5:1-21)

To live as a child of God means there will be attacks from the world. John wanted readers to walk in confidence through life, not based on their flesh, but based on the cross of Jesus.

6. Faithful to Truth (2 John)

In his second epistle John stressed there is an enemy out there, and his goal is to deceive us. We must be vigilant and faithful as we navigate the world.

7. Hospitable in Truth (3 John)

Hospitality is one of the best ways to demonstrate our love for God and His people. We must always be ready to receive and care for our brothers and sisters of the faith. By doing so we demonstrate our understanding of the truth.

Let's get started!

FELLOWSHIP WITH GOD

Relationships are important. In the movie *Cast Away*, Chuck Noland, played by Tom Hanks, is a FedEx executive. While en route to an assignment in Malaysia, his plane crashes somewhere in the south Pacific Ocean. Chuck survives the crash, but is washed up on the shore of a deserted island. Chuck makes several attempts to flee the island before eventually accepting his dilemma and beginning preparations to survive on the island. The island provides many of the elements necessary for survival, but it does not provide the one thing Chuck craves the most, relationship. Chuck becomes so lonely he makes his own companion out of a volleyball, whom he aptly names Wilson, that has washed up on shore.

All of us need relationships. We need other people, and most importantly we need God. When we are missing authentic relationships with God and others we, in our sin, create substitutes. Chuck missed real people to connect with on the island, so he created a pseudo friend in Wilson. We are no different. While we might be surrounded by people, we can still find ourselves alone in a crowd. John wrote about our need to be in right relationship with God and others. In his first letter, John reminded his readers that his purpose for writing them was so they would know the joy that comes from having fellowship with God. One of the great benefits of knowing God comes in the joy that fills our live through such a relationship.

PERSONAL TESTIMONY (1 JOHN 1:1-4)

John opened his letter by reminding his readers that he was writing to them about things he had actually seen, heard, and experienced during his years spent walking with Jesus. Many years had passed since John left his

Housing area in Capernaum. Capernaum is believed to have been the home of Peter, James, and John during the earthly ministry of Jesus. John later lived and ministered in Ephesus.

(ILLUSTRATOR PHOTO/ BOB SCHATZ (60/17/14)

fishing boat on the waters of the Sea of Galilee, but John never forgot what he heard. John not only described what he personally experienced during his three years of walking with Jesus, he also described what was revealed to him through the Holy Spirit about Jesus. Similar to the opening of his Gospel, John began his first letter by describing the eternal nature of Jesus. Knowing Jesus **was from the beginning,** and that He is **the word of life** are not things one comes to know simply by watching. Those are things that were revealed to John by listening to the Holy Spirit.

When we read that Jesus was **from the beginning,** it ought to draw our attention back to John's introductory words from his Gospel where he declared, "In the beginning was the Word, and the Word was with God, and the Word was God. He was with God in the beginning. All things were created through him, and apart from him not one thing was created that has been created" (John 1:1-3). The fact that John would return to the doctrine of the incarnation so early in his letter should tell us something important about what John wanted his readers to know about Jesus. Without the incarnation, without the Word becoming flesh, we would have no fellowship with God. Without the incarnation, John could never have written the phrase **concerning the word of life—that life was revealed.** Revealed!!! God has revealed Himself to us in the person of Jesus. Everything John would write to his readers is based on this amazing truth. Jesus has come, God has been revealed, and this changes everything.

When we want someone to remember something, we tell them more than once. People learn by repetition. This is especially true of our doctrine. There is a reason certain people can sing some of the old hymns from memory even though we have not heard many of them in years. For the first eighteen years of my life we sang the same fifty or so hymns every year. It was the repetition of hearing those songs over and over that caused those words and tunes to be seared into my mind and heart. Before John could make his argument for why **our joy may be complete** in Jesus, he needed to remind his readers again that Jesus transcended their circumstances. He was the incarnation of God. If our joy is made complete, then it has to be based on something, or in this case Someone, that is bigger than us. The incarnation teaches us that Jesus stands outside the circumstances of our lives. One of the hymns my church sang often was written by Edward Mote in 1834. He titled it, *My Hope Is Built on Nothing Less.* The first verse of that hymn says, "My hope is built on nothing less Than Jesus' blood and righteousness; I dare not trust the sweetest frame, But wholly lean on Jesus' name." Mote understood that our hope,

MY TESTIMONY

John's letter opened with the reminder that he had personally seen, heard, and known Jesus during the years spent as His follower. John's personal testimony was the basis for his letter and the authority with which he wrote.

Consider your own testimony about Jesus:

How has He revealed Himself to you?

How has He healed you?

How has He changed you?

How has He set you free?

How has He given you peace or direction?

How has He called you?

our life, our joy, must be built on something other than life's circumstances; it must be built on a relationship with Jesus—the incarnate One, who was, and is, and is to come.

FELLOWSHIP IN THE LIGHT (1 JOHN 1:5)

Those of us who have been married for very long can look back and see we have had some good times and times when we struggled. If we are honest, we can likely see that the times we struggled most were when we were out of fellowship with each other. A major reason we get out of fellowship is that we cease communicating well with each other. In some cases, we allow work or some other time consumer to take us away far too often. Other times circumstances around life take our attention away from each other. The result is frequently a breakdown in our communication and fellowship. When we are not listening well, we miss hearing about one another's joys, needs, concerns, and hurts. We might be in geographic proximity to one another, but we are not in fellowship with one another. If we Christians are going to walk in fellowship with God, we have to listen carefully to the message He has declared to us, and not just be in the proximity of the truth. In verse 5 John wrote that he was declaring **the message we have heard from him.** If we are going to have fellowship with God, it must begin by listening to His words through the Scripture.

In middle school my class took a field trip to Mammoth Cave, Kentucky. I apologize now to the middle-school teachers who went with our group on that trip. I am sure taking a few hundred kids safely into a dark cave took an immense amount of bravery and skill. As we navigated down into the cave, there was a section that opened up into a giant room. There were benches in the cavern, and our class was asked to sit as the park ranger gave a lesson on darkness. The ranger talked about ambient light, and how even in a dark room at our house or a dark night outside, some measure of light is still present. Then she turned off the lights in the cave so that we would experience total darkness. In my middle-school mind, I figured it couldn't be much different than I had experienced before on camping trips or in my room at home. I was wrong. When the lights went out, I couldn't see anything. Nothing! It was completely dark. This darkness lasted about one minute until a few of us middle-school boys figured out we could poke the people sitting in front of us and no one would know who it was. At that point the teachers asked the ranger to immediately turn the lights back on.

John used the motif of **light** and **darkness** to explain what fellowship with God looks like. However, instead of describing physical darkness like in a cave, John wrote that in Jesus there is no darkness at all. Whereas I could not see anything in that cave, through fellowship with God nothing can be hidden. There is only light, no darkness. These words are striking because John did not tell the reader God creates light or that He is similar to light. He said **God is light.** James Montgomery Boice noted that many biblical writers told us what God does, but John told us who God is. John wrote that God in His true nature is spirit (John 4:24), God is light (1 John 1:5), and God is love (4:8).[1] When we understand that God is light, we can see the impact of these words in John's Gospel, "This is the judgment: The light has come into the world, and people loved darkness rather than the light because their deeds were evil. For everyone who does evil hates the light and avoids it, so that his deeds may not be exposed" (John 3:19-20).

THE TRUTH ABOUT SIN (1 JOHN 1:6-10)

Many parents have had to deal with our kids telling lies. We might even know that what they are telling us is nowhere near the truth. In some cases, when we confront them, they tell more concoctions that deep down make us laugh. Have you ever wondered if God does not shake His head at some of the unbelievable things you and I do and say? Surely on some occasions He must be thinking, "You expect Me to believe that? I am the God of the universe. The One who never slumbers or sleeps. The One who knitted you together in your mother's womb, and you expect Me to believe that?" We might be able to hide some things about who we really are from other people, but we cannot hide anything from the all-knowing God. He knows when we walk in truth, but He knows when we don't as well. In the next section of text John exposed many of the lies we are apt to believe about our sin.

John used three **If we say** statements in verses 6-10 to demonstrate people's misunderstanding of how their sin impacts their fellowship with God. His primary reason for this was to correct the false teaching of the Gnostics. The Gnostics were a group of people who claimed to have a superior knowledge and fellowship with God. They believed they had a more enlightened understanding of God. John wrote to deconstruct or break down their arguments and in turn, he gave us a framework to examine our own hearts and lives.

Let's examine each of these claims. We will begin in verse 6 where John said, **If we say, "We have fellowship with him," and yet we walk in darkness, we are lying and are not practicing the truth.** John taught that people who truly know God and are in fellowship with Him, see the connection between belief and conduct. The type of life John was warning against is the person who has a practice of habitual and unrepentant sin. John did not imply that people never find themselves in dark moments of sin. We all fall short far more often than we would like to admit. What he taught was that walking in darkness is not a regular lifestyle for someone who experiences fellowship with God. The inverse of walking in regular habitual sin is to walk in the light. Those who walk in this manner will find the grace of God (the blood of Jesus, His Son, cleanses us from all sin) is readily available. This great news is that it frees us to be honest with ourselves, with others, and most importantly with God. Walking in the light does not mean we live a life absent of sin, it means we live a life confessing and repenting of it.

Following the first "if we say" statement, we see how John unpacked the benefits of walking in the light. The first benefit is we will be in right relationship with both God and others. Relationships are hard. They require patience and grace. God deeply cares about our relationships with other people. We cannot be in right fellowship with Him and be out of fellowship with others. Therefore, we should **walk in the light** not only before God, but also before others. The benefit in doing so is that we will experience the depths of His love and grace. Walking in fellowship with God and others is so important that John tied it to the cross itself. What Jesus did on the cross was to cleanse us. The great news from this text is that we can have fellowship with God through His Son Jesus. It does not matter what type of sin we have been involved in. Today you might be struggling with porn, or gossip. You might be having an affair or stealing from your company. Today you might be carrying the heavy burden of debilitating sins of years gone by, but the good news for you today is that through the sacrifice of Jesus you can be in fellowship with God. There is no better news than this.

The second use of the phrase "if we say" appears in verse 8. Here John confronted the Gnostics on another one of their claims. This claim was that it was possible to know God so well that we no longer sin. The Gnostics taught that it was possible to become so enlightened that one ceased to struggle with sin. They believed it was possible to achieve a level of perfection on earth. John wrote that followers of Christ ought to know better.

We ought not be **deceiving ourselves** by this. John wanted his readers to understand how pervasive our sin is. We no longer pursue its momentary pleasures as we learn to walk in the light, but it is not something we escape from in its entirety while living on earth. This ought to be a great encouragement to us. I have been a Christian for over thirty years, and while my

The Gnostics taught that it was possible to become so enlightened that one ceased to struggle with sin. They believed it was possible to achieve a level of perfection on earth. John wrote that followers of Christ ought to know better.

Below: Papyrii fragment containing the end of the Apocrypha of John and beginning of the Gospel of Thomas, two Gnostic texts. John wrote his epistles in part to combat Gnostic ideas and concepts.

desire is to walk in righteousness and faithfulness to God, there are still some places in my heart and life where I struggle—places where I must return to the well of His grace more frequently than I wish. As we follow Him, we need to be honest about our sin. If we do not understand the dangers of our sin, then we will not understand the power of Christ over it, and we will not be able to walk in right fellowship with God.

One of the dangers of misunderstanding sin comes when we fool ourselves into thinking that sin does not matter or that we can evade it. John Owen, the Puritan theologian, rightly described sin in this manner: "It has no doors to open. It needs no engine by which to work. It lies in the mind and in the understanding. It is found in the will. It is in the inclinations of the affections.... It has such intimacy in the soul."[2] Owen accurately described how sin so easily captures our affection. To faithfully oppose the false teaching of the Gnostics, John confronted the notion that it is possible to separate our fellowship with God from the patterns of our lives. If we fall for this lie, then we have deceived ourselves into believing like the world. The world teaches us that we are inherently good people who occasionally mess up. The Scripture teaches us that we are inherently sinful people separated from God, and that if it were not for the grace of God, lavishly poured out upon us through the person of Jesus, we would be separated from God and would have no fellowship with Him. The gospel calls us to daily die to self, repent of our sin, and lean into the grace of Jesus. Pretending not to struggle with sin leads us into darkness, hypocrisy, and a works-based theology; all of which lead to death.

So, how do we battle the sin in our lives? John showed us how in verse 9. The answer to sin in our lives is to expose it to the power of the cross (the light). We must **confess our sins** to Jesus and others who love the light. Confession is crucial to combating the false claim that we are without sin. When we confess our sin, we declare something great about the nature of God. First, we confess that He is **faithful** and second that He is **righteous.** If He were not both of these, then our sin would surely be the end of us, but because He has faithfully declared us righteous in the person of Jesus, we are made so. Second, God is just, so we can take comfort in the fact that the righteous judge has accepted the payment of Christ for our sin. So, in those attributes of His nature He demonstrates His mercy toward us in that He first will **forgive** us and second, He will **cleanse** us.

Let's examine how God responds to our confession through forgiveness. When God says He has forgiven us, He means that He no longer holds our sin against us. He has forgiven the debt we owe. However, there

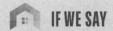

IF WE SAY

John used three "If we say" statements in 1 John 1:6-10 to demonstrate how a person's misunderstanding of sin impacts fellowship with God.

Reread each statement. Have you ever believed one of these lies? Prayerfully consider your own current relationship with God and whether or not you are believing false statements. Write a prayer in response to each of the passages.

If we say, "We have fellowship with him," and yet we walk in darkness, we are lying and are not practicing the truth.

If we say, "We have no sin," we are deceiving ourselves, and the truth is not in us.

If we say, "We have not sinned," we make him a liar, and his word is not in us.

is more to how God responds to our confession. He not only forgives, but He also cleanses us. This cleansing means we are no longer defiled by our sin. What has kept us separated from God has been removed. The tense of these two Greek words indicates that both the forgiveness and the cleansing are completed works. They are not an ongoing action. This work was already accomplished by Jesus on the cross and not caused by the confession itself.

The third "if we say" statement comes in verse 10. Here John exposed the worst lie we can believe about our sin. It is the lie that we have never sinned, specifically that **we have not sinned** after coming to faith in God. We actually find this to be the opposite in our own livves. The more deeply we walk with Jesus, the more sin we see in our own hearts. What makes this belief so dangerous is that when applied in our lives, it does not just make me a liar, but if it were true (which of course it is not) it makes God Himself a liar. For the Christ-follower, there are not many things we can say that are much worse. Paul said it this way in Romans 3:4, "Let God be true, even though everyone is a liar." These three "if we say" statements ought to serve as a checklist against a false understanding of our sin and God's grace toward us as sinners.

SIN AND THE GOSPEL (1 JOHN 2:1-2)

As we enter into the second chapter, John continued with an emphasis on how our fellowship with God is inseparable from the gospel itself. This is important because some may read the previous verses and see the gospel message and think that John was providing excuses for us when we sin. John wrote those words to push back against false teachers and to speak truth into the lives of those who desire to follow Jesus. In order to make sure his readers did not wrongly see his teaching as a license to sin, he concluded with these words: **My little children, I am writing you these things so that you may not sin.** In this statement we see the heart of a shepherd. John called his audience his **children**, indicating a natural love for them and a desire to see them grow in their knowledge and faith. However, he also strongly spoke truth into their lives by urging them to view the grace of God not as a license to sin, but as balm to brokenness from sin. He then finished this thought by pointing to the One who provides this truth and this grace, Jesus. Have you placed your trust in Him? If not, would you do so today?

A CLOSER LOOK

Propitiation

John used an interesting word in 1 John 2:2 to conclude this section. It is a word that is only found a handful of times in the New Testament. What makes it a difficult word for us is that we do not use it very often in our language. To rightly understand it and its significance, we need to take a closer look. The Greek word is translated in the Christian Standard Bible (and others) as "atoning sacrifice." In the King James (and others) it is rendered as "propitiation." The word literally can be defined as "the means by which sins are forgiven—'the means of forgiveness, expiation.'"[3]

This word also appears in Romans 3:25 where Paul wrote, "God presented him as the mercy seat (propitiation) of his blood, through faith, to demonstrate his righteousness, because in his restraint God passed over the sins previously committed." The mercy seat was the place in the Holy of Holies where the high priest on the annual Day of Atonement sprinkled the blood of the sacrificial lamb in pleading for the forgiveness of God's people. We can see by Paul's reference that he was also referring to the work of Jesus on the cross as the atoning sacrifice.

When we come across this word in the text, it ought to cause us to think about the means by which we can experience fellowship with God. The Scripture is clear, there is only one way that we can experience this forgiveness. God made it possible only through Jesus. Therefore, it is impossible to have fellowship with God without a relationship with His Son. This is true not only for us, but, as John wrote, also for those of the whole world.

Personal Reflection

1. All of us are people of relationship. If an outside observer studied your life, with whom or what would that person say your most important relationship is? Why would the observer conclude that? Would you agree with the observer's conclusion? If not, what do you need to change to cause your life to better reflect your valued relationships really are important?

2. How much of the joy you experience in life would you attribute to your fellowship with Jesus? Explain your answer.

3. What evidences of "light" and "darkness" do you see in the world around you? To what degree do you reflect that "God is light" to the world around you?

4. On a scale of 0 (never) to 10 (frequently), how regularly is confession of sin part of your devotion to God? Would your answer more nearly reflect an admission of sin or a deceiving of yourself about not having sin? Why?

1. J. M. Boice, *The Epistles of John, An Expositional. Commentary* (Grand Rapids: Baker Books, 1979), 28.

2. John Owen, *Triumph Over Temptation* (Colorado Springs: Victor, 2005), 47.

3. J. P. Louw and E. A. Nida, *Greek-English Lexicon of the New Testament Based on Semantic Domains,* Volume 1 (New York: United Bible Societies, 1988), 504.

REMAINING WITH GOD

1 JOHN 2:3-27

Before we were married and had children of our own, my wife's sister had a daughter. Therefore, as soon as I got married I, instantly became an uncle. Being an uncle is great because you can be super fun, and you don't have to change dirty diapers or discipline the kid. This then actually allows you to become the greatest person in the world to your niece or nephew. Thankfully, my niece and I developed a great relationship—so much so that she would come and spend several weeks at our house almost every summer. In many ways, we loved her like our own daughter. One of my favorite things about my niece was that she would repeat or do anything I said. If I told her to say something, she would say exactly that. She would use the same voice inflection and everything. She listened closely so she could repeat it back in an identical way. She was great at imitating people. She would try to say or do something exactly as you had modeled. It was like having a human parrot. This provided hours of endless entertainment for my wife and me.

Imitation can be one of the greatest forms of respect and honor. When we imitate someone, we are saying we like something about that person. We are saying we find that person worthy. In the text for this chapter, we are going to see that imitating Christ is what our lives should be about. If we really know and love Jesus, we will want our thoughts, speech, and lives to imitate Him. It is how we know we belong to Him. It is how we remain in a thriving relationship with Him.

RESPONDING TO DOUBTS (1 JOHN 2:3A)

I have been in vocational ministry for over twenty years, and I have seen a lot of changes in what people think about, struggle with, and question. However, there is one question that I hear as frequently today as I did twenty years ago. That question is, "How can I be sure that I am saved? I especially hear this question from adults who might have had an experience with God as a child but are now in the throes of life and are wondering if their encounter with Jesus and conversion was authentic. It is also often asked by those who thought they really knew Jesus but have made some very sad mistakes in life and have allowed sin to take root in their hearts. John addressed this

Below: The end of 2 Peter (3:16-18) and the beginning of 1 John (1:1–2:9) from Codex Alexandrinus (AD 400–440).

question head on in the second chapter of this letter. He wrote these words to provide both warning and encouragement.

In chapter 1, John grabbed the attention of the reader by repeating the phrase "if we say" to challenge the teachings of the Gnostics and to provide understanding into how sin impacts our fellowship with God. In chapter 2, he similarly used a phrase twice that he repeated throughout the remainder of the letter for emphasis: **This is how we know.** It is not hard to imagine the readers of John's letter asking the questions, "How can I know that I have fellowship with God? How can I know that I belong to Him?" John did not want to leave his readers guessing. He wanted them to know they could walk in full assurance and complete confidence with God. To help them, John provided an evaluation diagnostic. This evaluation tool has three components. The first is our obedience, the second is our love, and the third is our doctrine. By looking at our own lives through these three lenses, we can better measure whether we are in the faith.

KEEP HIS COMMANDS (1 JOHN 2:3B-6)

The first tool we can use to evaluate whether we are in fellowship with God is by asking the question, "Do we obey Him?" One way we can know we belong to Jesus is that **we keep his commands.** That sounds fairly simple, yet we just read in chapter 1 that anyone who says he no longer sins is a liar. So, if we sin by failing to keep His commands, are we no longer in Him? What did John mean when he said we must keep His commands. What commands was he talking about? There appears to be a lot for us to consider in these verses.

Having told his readers that obedience is a sure sign of fellowship with God, John then addressed those who claim to have fellowship, but have no interest in obeying God. Those who fall into this category John called liars. John then described the opposite type of person, the one who is in right fellowship with God. These are the ones he described as keepers of the word. They are not liars, but they instead walk in truth. Walking in truth means they desire to imitate the obedience of Christ.

LOVE OTHERS (1 JOHN 2:7-17)

The second component of the test is our love for others. When Jesus talked about the law as recorded in the Gospels, it was usually in the context of how do we love God and others. In fact, Matthew 22:37-39 records that

KNOW THAT YOU KNOW

In 1 John 2, John answered the question: "How can I know that I am saved?" with three statements:

1. "The one who says, 'I have come to know him,' and yet doesn't keep his commands, is a liar, and the truth is not in him" (v. 4).

How committed are you to keeping His commands? Are there commands you disregard?

2. "The one who says he remains in him should walk just as he walked" (v. 6).

In what ways does your everyday life (your "walk") look like Jesus'?

3. "The one who says he is in the light but hates his brother or sister is in the darkness .... The one who loves his brother or sister remains in the light" (vv. 9-10).

Are each of your relationships marked by love for others? Have you fooled yourself into thinking you love when it's not genuine?

Jesus told us to "'Love the Lord your God with all your heart, with all your soul, and with all your mind. This is the greatest and most important command. The second is like it: Love your neighbor as yourself.'" Jesus followed this summary statement with the additional declaration, "'all the Law and the Prophets depend on these two commands'" (v. 40). What He indicated is that we will be following the commands of God if we will do these two things well. The concept of loving our neighbor well is not limited to this text. In John 13:34-35 Jesus said that He was giving a new command. This new command dovetails with the text previously mentioned. In it Jesus said "'I give you a new command: Love one another. Just as I have loved you, you are also to love one another. By this everyone will know that you are my disciples, if you love one another.'"

The Scripture is crystal clear on what the commands of Jesus are to those who are in fellowship with Him. We are to love. Therefore, one of the ways we can determine if we are in fellowship with God is by evaluating the way we love God and others. Do we treasure God? Do we long to know Him more and spend time with Him? When couples first start dating, they look forward to every second they can spend together, eagerly anticipating the times when they can go out together. When they are not together, they often are thinking about the next time they will be able to see each other. They have a genuine affection and love to see and be near the other. While those thoughts and feeling take new shapes and forms after many years of marriage,many still say that when they are away from each other, they are always eager to get home and see one another again. There is a real affection and desire to be in relationship together. Our love for God can also be measured by our desire to think on Him, to pray, to spend time in His presence. It is also measured by the way we care for, serve, and treat others.

When we arrive at verses 12-14, we see a slight change in the style and intention of John's letter. He had been addressing those who needed to re-examine whether or not they were in Christ. When he penned these next verses, it feels as if he wanted to make sure that he took a moment to affirm those who were doing it right so that it would not cause unnecessary concern for those who were faithfully walking in that love. Therefore, he singled out different groups of people within the church who were imitating well the love of the Son. He included **little children, fathers,** and **young men.** It is most likely that John used these titles to describe spiritual maturity, not biological ages. To the younger or new believers (little children) he reminded them of the most basic gospel truth—in Christ we find forgiveness for sin. To the more mature (fathers), he reminded them of their deep love and knowledge of the faith. To the spiritually growing and energetic (young men), he reminded them that through Christ they were more than conquerors. Sometimes as we teach and lead people, it is good to remind them of who they are and where they are seeing spiritual progress. John needed to make sure those who were walking in the faith were affirmed and praised before he returned to challenging those who might not have been founded in Christ.

Unrivaled Affections (vv. 15-17)

In verses 15-17, John returned to a position of warning. He offered an imperative command for the believer that we should not love the things the world loves. If our citizenship is in a different place (heaven) than the world, then the pleasures of this world should not compete for our attention and affection. This is certainly an aspect of our lives that God is still working on. In our minds and hearts, we do not want to have affection for the world. We do not want to have **the lust of the flesh** or **of the eyes.** Our desire is for our hearts and minds to be pure. We do not want to have **pride** in **possessions** or positions. We want to love the things of the kingdom and not the things of this world, but in our flesh there are still moments that we find ourselves chasing the fleeting pleasures of this world. The good news in this particular text is that John told his readers why they should not pursue the things of the flesh, so we can find our encouragement and motivation in it as well. If we look at verse 17, we can almost hear John warn his readers that the things of this world are **passing away.** The things we look at with lust, the things we think of that are fleeting, the objects or possessions that we boast about owning or controlling, they will all be gone. They will not last. The only thing that is eternal is our life investment in the kingdom. So, if we invest ourselves in God's kingdom, if we commit our souls to the King, we will live with Him forever.

LOVE TRUTH (1 JOHN 2:18-27)

The third component of evaluation that John gave his readers was to measure their love of the truth. I grew up in a time and context where there was a great emphasis on the end times or last days. This meant that there was a lot of discussion about the concept of the antichrist. Any discussion of this was usually accompanied by a series of charts and graphs about the return of Jesus. The topic of the end times is often used to strike fear into the hearts of people. The emotions those thoughts produce are usually rooted in trying to understand our position before God. Are we saved? If Jesus comes back today, will I be ready? John began this section of his letter by telling us that the **last hour** is here. When people say we are living in the end times, this is true. However, it might be important to note that we have been living in the last hour for nearly two thousand years. The doctrines that John explained in this text are not new for today, but they have been true since the Holy Spirit inspired John to write them down.

Who Are the Antichrists? (vv. 18-23)

Let us begin our look at this section of text by noting a few things John told his readers about **antichrist.** First, John told us that there is not just one antichrist who is currently somewhere in the world devising a plan to take over the world and bring an evil reign of terror down upon God's people. There has been quite a bit of emphasis in the past few decades looking for the one person and trying to figure out who this person might be. The discussion of end times, and specifically talk about the antichrist, were often used to strike fear in the hearts of people about whether or not they were saved or if they were living for God. For some time there were conferences and articles published where the goal was to try to identify who the antichrist was or if he was currently alive and preparing his eventual reign of terror.

John, however, told his readers several interesting things about this subject. For one, there are **many antichrists.** Often, we think only of one antichrist coming near the return of Christ, but John taught that there were many who had already come and many more who were coming. This raises the important question then of what is an antichrist? The expression *antichrist* can imply two things. First, the Greek prefix *anti* can mean "in place of," so *antichrist* could be one claiming to be in place of Christ. Second, *anti* also can mean "against, opposed to, opposite," implying one who opposed or was the opposite of Christ. Both definitions can be applied here. One whom John described as an antichrist is both someone who may claim to be Jesus and someone who is instead the exact opposite of Jesus.

Another thing John taught about the antichrists is that often they might initially appear to be one of us. He told his readers **they went out from us.** This indicates that for a period of time they might seem as sound in doctrine as true believers. There might be some within our own camps who at the present time we believe to be teachers and followers of Jesus,

WHAT DOES IT SAY?

First John 2:18-23 may seem daunting or even confusing. However, we have God's Holy Word coupled with the Holy Spirit, who teaches us what we need to know about the Bible.

Carefully consider the three terms below. From the text, write all you observe about what IS and what IS NOT in John's passage.

last hour (v. 18)
Is:

Is not:

antichrist(s) (vv. 18,22)
Is:

Is not:

truth (vv. 20-21)
Is:

Is not:

but in time they will depart from the doctrine of truth and promote a false gospel that elevates their own lives and views over those of Jesus. Paul warned the elders in Ephesus of something similar. In Acts 20:29-31 he told them, "after my departure savage wolves will come in among you, not sparing the flock. Men will rise up even from your own number and distort the truth to lure the disciples into following them. Therefore be on the alert, remembering that night and day for three years I never stopped warning each one of you with tears." Later, he would warn Timothy, "For the time will come when people will not tolerate sound doctrine, but according to their own desires, will multiply teachers for themselves because they have an itch to hear what they want to hear. They will turn away from hearing the truth and will turn aside to myths" (2 Tim. 4:3-4).

Throughout the Scripture there are important warnings about those who would come in to teach falsely and set themselves up as "wolves" among sheep. Even in this, we see the concept of the prefix *anti* demonstrated. Jesus came as the Lamb of God (John 1:29). What is often viewed as the opposite of a lamb, but a wolf? It is in the arrival of these wolves or antichrists that we can know with certainty that it is the last hour. It was not only their teaching that revealed that they were not in the faith, but it was also the fact they refused to remain a part of the community of believers. John proclaimed that **they went out from us, but they did not belong to us; for if they had belonged to us, they would have remained with us.** One of the most important ways our doctrine is shaped is by living in community with other believers. Being a member of a local church is so vital for our spiritual health and growth. It is within that community of believers that we can be encouraged and corrected. Those who refuse (like the false teachers/antichrists) do not desire to walk in the light that the community of local believers provides. They do not desire to have their lives inspected or corrected.

John also identified the markers of an antichrist. Such an antichrist will be a **liar** and **one who denies that Jesus is the Christ.** They will not recognize Jesus as the Messiah who was sent from the Father. For us it is important that we walk in right doctrine. While there are certainly areas of doctrine where there is room for disagreement on how to rightly apply the truth through application, there are certain doctrines that we must hold on to tightly or we do not hold the faith at all. Someone who is in Christ and has salvation must hold an unshakable belief in the truth that Jesus is the Christ, the Son of the Living God. Anyone who denies this truth cannot belong to Him and has no fellowship with God.

Below: Herodian lamp from 37 BC to AD 70. The body and nozzle were made separately and later attached. These lamps are usually found in Judea, making it likely they were mainly used by Jews. John used the image of light versus darkness in 1 John 1:5-7; 2:8-10.

Being a member of a local church is so vital for our spiritual health and growth. It is within that community of believers that we can be encouraged and corrected. Those who refuse (like the false teachers/antichrists) do not desire to walk in the light . . .

Remaining with God (vv. 24-27)

Followers of Christ must hold to faithful obedience, abiding love, and right doctrine. These three marks will help confirm one's position in Christ. This will allow us to examine our lives and see if we are in the faith (2 Cor. 13:5). The reward for this is the promise of eternal life that we can find only through fellowship with Jesus. John concluded this portion of his letter be calling readers back to these basic concepts. He told them to **remain** in these so that they could rest in the assurance of their faith. While there are many in the world who will try to distract our hearts and minds from these truths, John urged his readers not to become distracted. Focusing our affection and attention on these truths allows us not only to be in fellowship with God, but to remain rooted deeply in Him!

A CLOSER LOOK

Remain or Abide

John placed significant emphasis on what it looks like to **remain** or abide in Christ. The word in the Greek literally means "to remain in the same place over a period of time— 'to remain, to stay.'"[1] John's emphasis on this was not new to this letter. It is something he heard directly from the Master Himself. In his Gospel, John recorded the words of Jesus on this subject. The timing in which Jesus offered these words is important. He shared this truth in chapter 15 immediately following the washing of the disciples' feet and immediately before He took them to the garden of Gethsemane where Jesus would be betrayed and arrested. Jesus knew that there would be a lot of doubt in the hearts and minds of His disciples when this happened, so He took time to reassure them about who He is and who they were when they abided or remained in Him. Read closely John 15:1-17 and see the similarities in the way John recorded the teachings of Jesus and how he shared those truths many years later with the recipients of his first letter. One thing to pay close attention to is how remaining in Jesus is so closely associated with how we love people. Perhaps abiding in Him is how we can love people who are difficult to love. It is not our love, but it is allowing the love of God to flow through us to others. There have been several times in my life when I knew I needed to love someone who was very difficult. In those times all I could say to God was, "God help me to love You and remain in You so that You can demonstrate Your love through me to this person." Every single time I have prayed that prayer, God has given me a capacity to love people that I could never muster up in my own strength.

Personal Reflection

1. Has there been a time in your life when you doubted your salvation? Describe it. What caused your doubt? Does the doubt linger? If not, how did you receive the reassurance you sought?

2. Which of the three tests in 1 John 2 do you think is the most applicable to addressing your doubts and why?

3. Why was it appropriate for John to be so concerned about false teachers? How can we identify false teaching today? Where do you see examples of such false teaching in our time?

4. Why is remaining in Christ important ? How can we walk in that truth? On a scale of 0 (completely forsaking Christ) to 10 (remaining in Him in every way possible), how fully do you remain in Christ? Why did you rate yourself as you did? If Christ would not be satisfied with the level of your remaining in Him, what will you do to more fully abide in Him?

1. J. P. Louw and E. A. Nida, *Greek-English Lexicon of the New Testament Based on Semantic Domains*, Volume 1 (New York: United Bible Societies, 1988), 729.

LIVING AS GOD'S CHILDREN

1 JOHN 2:28–3:10; 4:1-6

How will you feel when Jesus returns? Will you walk with confidence or will you want to hide your head in shame? When I was a child, I did and said something I am not proud of. I was not an awful child, but I certainly tested my parents' patience at times. When I was in elementary school, I had a teacher who would grade our work then ask us to go home and have our parents sign the papers so that she could know we had shown them our work. On one of these assignments I did not prepare adequately. Therefore, I did not receive a very good grade. I knew I had messed up because I had not told my parents about the assignment, and I had not performed well on it. At the same time, I did not want to get in trouble at home for not preparing and taking my school assignment seriously. So, I devised a plan in an attempt to escape punishment. My plan was to bring up cursive handwriting in a casual conversation with my parents and to trick my mother into signing her name on a blank sheet of paper. I would then take that paper and write a note on the top saying that I had lost the assignment and that I had instead told her about my grade. The first part of my plan was executed to perfection. I now had a blank piece of notebook paper with my mother's signature about halfway down. I took that paper, wrote my grade and note about losing it, and turned it in to my teacher. This is where my plan fell apart. The next day my teacher called me to her desk and asked me if I had really told my mother about the test score. I knew I was busted, so I confessed. She then handed me the note and told me to show my parents what I had done and to bring back a real note confirming that they had not only seen my grade, but also my confession. I was ashamed. As soon as my mom picked me up from school that afternoon, I burst into tears. I was ashamed of my grade and even more ashamed of how I had tried to deceive my parents. The reality for us is that our sin will always tell on us. Our sin will always bring us shame, but when we walk in the truth, God will restore us and cause us to walk in His grace.

PART OF THE FAMILY (1 JOHN 2:28–3:3)

In this section of the text, John provided instruction to his readers about how to live as God's children. In the first verse he began by providing direction that would allow believers to **not be ashamed** when Jesus returns. Instead of shame, John wanted his spiritual children to walk in the **confidence** that comes from being found in Him.

What will our lives look like if we abide in Him? The first thing that will become evident is that we will pursue that which is **righteous.** The Gnostics believed a person's spirit and soul were essentially good and that our spirits were protected from our outward bodies, which were evil. Therefore, they claimed to have a deep knowledge of God, but continued to flaunt their sinful behavior. They were unashamed. John repeatedly identified this as flawed doctrine. He concluded this section of his letter by recapping the argument he has made throughout the first two chapters: **Everyone who does what is right has been born of him.**

If there is a more encouraging verse than 3:1 in John's first letter I am not sure what it would be. John reminded his readers that **the Father** has

PUBLIC DOMAIN

The first stanza of John Newton's classic hymn, "Amazing Grace" reminds us that God has poured out His amazing grace to "save a wretch like me." This is what I think about when I look at John's words in 3:1.

Left: Before John Newton (1725-1807) became an Anglican minister and wrote the hymn, "Amazing Grace," he was a slave ship master. His conversion came at sea when caught in a severe storm and he feared he and his ship might sink.

During Jesus' crucifixion, He declared John to be Mary's adopted son. John later went to Ephesus where he worked and finally died. It is assumed he brought Mary with him. Shown is the so-called "House of St. Mary" at Ephesus. The house actually dates from the Byzantine Era to the 13th century.

ILLUSTRATOR PHOTO/ TOM HOOKE (66/6/03)

unfathomable love toward those who belong to Him. The very fact He would save sinners like us, then call us His own should never be lost on us. It ought to amaze us every day just like it amazed us the first day we heard it. When I read this verse, I always think about John Newton's classic hymn, "Amazing Grace." The first stanza reminds us that God has poured out His amazing grace to "save a wretch like me." This is what I think about when I look at John's words in 3:1. It is amazing to be part of the family of God—to **be called God's children**—and just in case we forget, John added the phrase **and we are!**

I have four children—one daughter and three sons. My wife and I adopted our three sons from China. They obviously do not look anything like me physically. Most of the time I forget about this fact, but every once in a while I am reminded, usually in a humorous way. Last year I was volunteering with my middle son's school. We were going on a field trip to a farm. When we got on the bus, my son was sitting next to one of his school friends. I had never met this friend, so he had no idea who I was. My son leaned over to inform the boy that his dad was on the trip. I saw this boy sit up and begin to look around. After scanning the bus for potential candidates, the boy said, "I don't see your dad." My son pointed to me (I sat in the seat across the aisle listening to this conversation) and said, "He is right there." The boy was now completely confused. He pointed at me and said, "Right there?" to which my son nodded. The friend then emphatically looked at my son and said, "He doesn't look like you."

The reason my son's classmate did not know to look for someone like me is because he did not really know my son. He did not know my son was born in China or that he was adopted. Had he known some of my son's background, then he perhaps would not have been so surprised to learn I was my son's dad. John wrote that the reason the world does not recognize Jesus is that they do not truly know Him. Never underestimate the importance of knowing Jesus. It is through faith in Him that we become His children … **and we are!**

John then turned his writing to address what will motivate us as we wait for Jesus' return. In 1 John 3:2-3 John told his audience that although we are presently **God's children,** we are not yet **what we will be.** There is a massive transformation coming for us. When Jesus appears we will see Him, not as He was in His earthly form, and not by faith alone, but we will see Him in all His glory. While we wait for this amazing moment, we are not to sit around in our sin, but to do our part in the process of sanctification (becoming more like Him). This includes the pursuit of purity. While we eagerly await His return, we must practice what Paul wrote in Philippians 4:8, "Whatever is true, whatever is honorable, whatever is just, whatever is pure, whatever is lovely, whatever is commendable—if there is any moral excellence and if there is anything praiseworthy—dwell on these things."

LEAVING OUR SIN BEHIND (1 JOHN 3:4-6)

In verse 4 John returned to the primary point of discussion for this part of his letter, the connection between being a child of God and having the conduct of a child of God. When I was a kid and I got in trouble, one of the things my parents would often say to me is, "Your last name is Keck, and Kecks do not do" whatever it was I had just done. This was their way of saying because I bore their last name, there would be requirements on what I could say or do. John reminded his readers that they bore the name of Jesus. The way they lived directly reflected what they believed about Christ.

LEAVING SIN BEHIND

Claiming to be sinless is lying to ourselves and others; we simply cannot do it. However, we can choose to strive to live according to God's standards of love and obedience, allowing our sin to break our hearts and send us to our knees.

Consider one sin that has been a struggle for you recently. Briefly describe it:

How has this sin affected your relationship with the Lord?

Have you confessed your sin? Write a prayer of confession here:

What Scriptures encourage you or keep you focused on maintaining your faithfulness to God in this area?

How has your worship kept you dependent on Christ for His strength to overcome your sin?

Believers are to actively be on guard, diligently watching for those who may be out to deceive them. . . . We must be watchful both of people in the world, but also of our enemy the devil.

Above: A 13th century wall painting fragment depicts demons carrying their prey hanging from a pole. This type of demon originated in Egypt and is connected with vegetation rituals.

ILLUSTRATOR PHOTO/ G.B. HOWELL/ ATHENS ARCHAEOLOGICAL MUSEUM (35/3/79)

The way John wrote about **sin** and **lawlessness** in verses 4-6 requires us to dive a little deeper. While there is some debate over these verses regarding exactly what John meant here, it is safe to conclude that any sin we commit breaks the law of God. This puts us clearly in the camp of being a lawbreaker. However, John appeared to be alluding to something even more. He had already declared that anyone who claims to be without sin is lying (1:6,8,10), so what did he mean when he said **everyone who remains in him does not sin?** The verb tenses indicate a distinction between the breaking of law and those who willingly walk in rebellion against God. For those who are in Christ, there ought to be a disgust toward sin. When we sin, it ought to break our own hearts. If our motives and desires are to continue to walk in sin with no regard to repentance, then that ought to raise concern regarding our position in Christ. At the same time, we should not read this text to mean that if we ever sin then we are not in Christ, or that we can lose our security in Christ. While there is much debate about the specific meaning of verses 4-6, for the believer we should only become alarmed when we begin to love our sin instead of repenting of it.

WHO IS YOUR FATHER? (3:7-10)

Have you ever been deceived? When I was a teenager one of the things my friends and I loved to do was to play practical jokes on each other. We took great pride in figuring out new ways to scare each other or put each other in awkward positions. Part of every great practical joke involves the art of deception. Deception often involves allowing your victim to be in a place of comfort or trust. Once they allow their guard down, you can follow through on the joke. Sadly, we have an enemy who is not trying to deceive us as a practical joke. He is out for our destruction, and it is no laughing matter. John has already warned his readers of this in 2:26 when he noted, "I write these things to you concerning those who are trying to deceive you." However, he became even more emphatic in his warning here in 3:7. John wrote **let no one deceive** with a present active imperative verb, which means this is a command. Believers are to actively be on guard, diligently watching for those who may be out to deceive them, including the previously mentioned antichrists (2:18). This is an important warning for us as well. If we are going to live as God's children, we too must be watchful. We must be watchful both of people in the world, but also of our enemy the devil.

John directed his readers to consider their lives in light of whom they belong to. If they belong to God, then their lives will reflect the righteousness of Christ. But if they continue to walk in darkness, then their true father is actually the devil. Many of us carry the traits of our parents. Perhaps we look like them, act like them, or speak like them. The reason for this is that we carry their DNA and have been influenced by their training during our upbringing. It is the same with our heavenly Father. The more time we spend with Him, the more we begin to think and talk like Him. However, this has not always been the case. We were not born into Christ at our physical birth, but rather we have been adopted into His family through faith in Jesus. When we were born, we were born in our sin and we were children of the world, where Satan is prince. Therefore, those not adopted into God's family through grace are children of the flesh and do not think or act like God. John called his readers to consider whom they take after. Did their lives reflect the fact that they had entered the family of God through faith? Or did their lives reflect that they were still lost in their sin? In verses 9-10, John wrote about being **born** and being born again or **born of God.** Here again we see John used similar language to what we find in his Gospel. It is hard to read these verses and not think back on the conversation Jesus had with Nicodemus in John 3, when the discussion of being born again was highlighted (John 3:3-7). In this letter, John gave us a clear picture of the way those who have been born again ought to live their lives.

TEST EVERYTHING (1 JOHN 4:1-6)

The instruction John gave to his readers in the first verses of chapter 4 are wise words for us today. There are still many ways that people are deceived, even a couple thousand years after John wrote his letter. Therefore, testing **every spirit** is vital in order for us to know if they are trustworthy and from God. We must never forget that we have an enemy who is a deceiver (Rev. 12:9). This means our battle for right discernment is a spiritual one. Our enemy is crafty and smooth, and he loves it when we fail to decipher the difference between the truth and his lies.

Have you or a friend ever watched an ad for something on television and purchased the item, thinking it would do for you what it supposedly did for the person in the ad? My roommate in college purchased an exercise machine that was frequently advertised on TV. The ad repeatedly claimed that if you used this machine just fifteen minutes a day, you would be in great shape. The commercial depicted several men and women using the machine—and of course their bodies looked fit and tone. I decided to give it a try. For almost three months I used that machine well past the fifteen minutes the ad suggested. After the first month I began to think the ad was an exaggeration, and after two months I knew it was. There was no way using that machine for fifteen minutes a day was going to make me look like the people in the commercial. By using the machine for several months, it was put to the test. It did not pass the test. It did not produce the fruit in my body that it had promised. As we get older and a bit wiser, we are able to see through many of the marketing ads because we understand more about how advertisers are trying to persuade us and how they are attempting to play to certain emotions. A little more research initially and neither I nor my roommate might not have fallen for the product back then either. This is similar to our spiritual journey. The longer we walk with Jesus and become knowledgeable about His Word, the greater our ability to rightly **test the spirits.** Hopefully we do not need to fall for

THE SPIRIT TEST

In 1 John 4:1-6, John instructed believers to "test the spirits to see if they are from God" (v. 1). What might a spiritual test look like?

Consider each of the following statements, asking yourself whether each confesses Jesus or comes from the world. Then add a few statements you've heard lately, analyzing their truthfulness in the same manner.

Statement: "It's my body; I can do what I want."
Worldly Belief Reflected:

Truth from God's Word:

Statement: "Since this only involves me, no one else is harmed."
Worldly Belief Reflected:

Truth from God's Word:

Statement: "Truth is situational; there are times when lying is appropriate."
Worldly Belief Reflected:

Truth from God's Word:

the temptations of the devil only to find out later the truth that he lied to us. If the marketing people can convince people to purchase insignificant things, then imagine what Satan is able to convince us of regarding the things of life. So, how can we test these spirits **to see if they are from God** or from the devil?

John gave us the first test. Does the person declare that Jesus is the Messiah, the Son of the Living God? If so, we can consider that person's testimony. If not, we can dismiss the testimony. During the first century, this was an important indicator of whether someone was of God. As we think about this test today, we need to remember that there was no written New Testament as we know it today when John wrote these letters. There was no constant source of written truth for believers to study. Today we have some additional ways we can test the spirits. For us, after we test whether or not a person believes Jesus is the Messiah, we can test his or her words against the plumb line of God's truth, the Bible. When we hear someone claim something is true, our first thought ought to be, "Does that line up with what the Scripture says?" If it does, then we can proceed to think on the claim and consider its relevancy and application in our lives. If it cannot be verified by Scripture, or contradicts Scripture, we can dismiss it as from the deceiver and react accordingly.

This might seem like a daunting task. How can I know? What if the deceiver is smarter than I am? What if he is craftier than I am? John must have understood that his readers would have some of the same questions. Therefore, he encouraged his readers (and us today) by reminding them that they had not been left to figure this out on their own. Believers have been given a powerful resource inside them that can help them to understand truth and walk in wisdom—the Holy Spirit. We have already overcome **the antichrist** and the deceivers of this world because we are in Christ, and Christ is victorious over these through His death, burial, and resurrection. John continued this line of reasoning by again reminding his readers, and us today, that we belong to God. We are His children. People who belong to God hear His voice and listen to Him; those who are of the world have the ears of those who walk in the ways of the world. This is in line with the words of Jesus recorded by John in his Gospel, "My sheep hear my voice, I know them, and they follow me" (John 10:27). It is clear that John placed great importance on the ability of a Christ-follower to discern through the Holy Spirit what is truth from the deception of the antichrists, false teachers, and ultimately the devil himself.

A CLOSER LOOK

Spirit of Deception

John used an interesting phrase in 1 John 4:6, "the spirit of deception." In context John said: "We are from God. Anyone who knows God listens to us; anyone who is not from God does not listen to us. This is how we know the Spirit of truth and the spirit of deception." The phrase, "the spirit of deception" is used nowhere else in the New Testament. The closest things we can find to it is found in 1 Timothy 4:1 where Paul mentioned "deceitful spirits." Both John and Paul indicated that there are two spirits active in the world today, "the Spirit of truth and the spirit of deception" (1 John 4:6). The first is from God, the second from Satan. Those who belong to God will hear and listen to God's Spirit of truth, just as those who belong to the world will hear and follow the spirit of deception. Sometimes it can be difficult to discern the difference, because the communicator may have the appearance of truth and yet not be found in it. The Spirit of truth will always elevate the person and name of Jesus and will be consistent with the Scripture. The spirit of deception will elevate self and proclaim a new freedom or knowledge that is rooted in our desire to sin without consequence. Paul also emphasized this in his letter to the church at Corinth when he wrote: "Now we have not received the spirit of the world, but the Spirit who comes from God, so that we may understand what has been freely given to us by God. We also speak these things, not in words taught by human wisdom, but in those taught by the Spirit, explaining spiritual things to spiritual people. But the person without the Spirit does not receive what comes from God's Spirit, because it is foolishness to him; he is not able to understand it since it is evaluated spiritually. The spiritual person, however, can evaluate everything, and yet he himself cannot be evaluated by anyone. For who has known the Lord's mind, that he may instruct him? But we have the mind of Christ" (1 Cor. 2:12-16).

Personal Reflection

1. In what areas of your life do you see the family resemblance to Christ most obviously?

2. Have you ever been broken over your own sin? If, so how did you respond?

3. Describe a time when you were deceived by someone, and how you discovered it.

4. When have you had to "test the spirits"? Describe the experience. What confirmed for you the truth or deception in that instance?

LIVING WITH LOVE

1 JOHN 3:11-24; 4:7-21

ove is a funny word in the English language. We use it in a variety of different ways. We can say, "I love ice cream," or we can say, "I love my children." The English language does not have a very good way of distinguishing the degrees by which we express this affection. To understand what love is we could go to one of the more popular texts in Scripture, 1 Corinthians 13, or we can take a deep dive in 1 John 3. As John's letter continued, he leaned further into the church on why they should practice love above all things. He reminded them again of this theme that runs through his entire letter, that they love one another. Before unpacking what love ought to look like, John gave an example of what it should never look like. Sometimes understanding what something does not look like can help us to see it for what it really is.

WHAT LOVE IS NOT (1 JOHN 3:11-15)

John returned to the Old Testament in order to demonstrate to his readers what love is not. He drew from the narrative of Cain and Abel in Genesis 4. It is in this text where we are introduced to these two sons of Adam and Eve. Cain was in the agricultural trade. He worked the ground (farmer). Abel was in the livestock field and tended to animals (shepherd/rancher). On one occasion it was decided they would bring an offering to the Lord (we are not told why). Cain brought some of the produce he had grown, and Abel brought the firstborn from his flock as an offering. After they gave their offerings, the Scripture says, "The LORD had regard for Abel and his offering, but he did not have regard for Cain and his offering" (Gen. 4:4-5). We are not told exactly why God rejected Cain's offering

Above: This Medieval ivory carving depicts Genesis 4:2-4, describing the offerings to God made by the sons of Adam and Eve. At top center, God's hand reaches from a cloud to bless Abel, left, shown holding a lamb. Cain and his offering of a sheaf of wheat at right are not blessed. John used Cain and Abel to portray evil and righteousness.

Cain's deeds were evil, but Abel's were righteous. That jealousy led to anger that ultimately led Cain to murder his brother in a field. John used this example to show believers how not to walk. . . . Rather, John told the church to love one another.

(we will explore some potential explanations in A Closer Look), but it must have been something about the offering itself, how it was offered, or Cain himself that did not please God (v. 7). John affirmed this account by describing Cain's deeds as evil. One additional insight we may glean here from John is that jealousy appeared to be involved in Cain's motive to murder his brother. Cain's **deeds were evil,** but Abel's **were righteous.** That jealousy led to anger that ultimately led Cain to murder his brother in a field. John used this example to show believers how not to walk. We are not to walk in faithless disobedience like Cain. We are not to let jealousy and anger take root in our hearts. We are not to express that anger through violence. Rather, John told the church to **love one another.** He then compared Cain and Abel to the world. **The world** is like Cain. Those in it live in disobedience to God. They walk without faith. They walk in darkness. Those of us who are in Christ are in the light. Thus we walk faithfully

48

in the truth like Abel. John informed his readers that they should **not be surprised.** They should not be caught off guard when their values and beliefs are despised by the world.

Several years ago, right after the United States Supreme Court issued a ruling with which I and many believers strongly objected, I posted something on social media indicating I was disappointed in the ruling. The source of my disappointment was my firm belief in the Bible teachings on the matter. It did not take long for many people to comment on my post. While some were in agreement, there were also many of my friends, who do not follow Christ, who vehemently disagreed. Almost immediately some began to call me names and speak very unkind things about me, my family, my church, and my values. During that moment the Lord brought 1 John 3:13 to my mind, **Do not be surprised, brothers and sisters, if the world hates you.** I was reminded that the world hates the truth because it first hated Jesus who is the Truth. John wrote this very thing in his Gospel, "This is the judgment: The light has come into the world, and people loved darkness rather than the light because their deeds were evil. For everyone who does evil hates the light and avoids it, so that his deeds may not be exposed" (John 3:19-20). When we walk with Jesus, the world will hate us, but their hate toward us should not deter our love for them. If we are to pursue being like Jesus, we must walk as He walked, and He repeatedly demonstrated love toward those who hated Him. In fact, He died for those who hated Him: "But God proves his own love for us in that while we were still sinners, Christ died for us" (Rom. 5:8).

John continued his letter here by returning to an earlier theme; if we really belong to God, we will love like Him. The mark of someone who is actually born again is that they **love our brothers and sisters.** One who does not love, does not have eternal life because that person **remains in death.** Such a one is like Cain the murderer, having a love of self and a love of the world that stirs up jealousy, anger, and hatred. John gave a strong warning to those who do not demonstrate love well.

WHAT LOVE IS (1 JOHN 3:16-18)

Many kids are great at making promises. They constantly tell us they are "about to do" something they have been asked to do. If told, "Go brush your teeth," they say, "I am about to." If asked if they have completed their homework they say, "I am about to." Everything is about what they are going to do and not much about what they are actually doing (or have already done).

We are also pretty good at using this line of reasoning with God. (He is not impressed with it any more than we parents are when our children use it.) We are always about to start that new devotion time or about to help that person in need. We are always planning and only occasionally completing. John wrote that love is not displayed in hollow words and promises; true love is displayed **in action and in truth.** As my mom always reminds me, "Actions speak louder than words."

After explaining in great lengths what love is not, John gave us another picture from Scripture. While Cain displayed what love is not, Jesus demonstrated what love is. John began by noting that the only way we can know real love is to turn our eyes upon Jesus. He is the definition of what real love looks like. Jesus did not just talk about His deep love for us, He demonstrated it when **He laid down his life for us.** His willingness to go to the cross and to die in our place shows us what love is. Paul reminded the church at Ephesus of this great love when he wrote, "But God, who is rich in mercy, because of his great love that he had for us, made us alive with Christ even though we were dead in trespasses" (Eph. 2:4-5). His love for us is the very basis for His action. In fact, John remembered a conversation Jesus had about the love the Father has for us in that famous interaction at night with Nicodemus. He recorded that interaction in John 3. Jesus declared, "For God loved the world in this way: He gave his one and only Son, so that everyone who believes in him will not perish but have eternal life" (John 3:16). John put the exclamation on this thought when he said, **We should also lay down our lives for our brothers and sisters.** However, this raises an important question. Obviously, Jesus' death was unique in every way, while we will never die to pay for the sins of our brothers and sisters (and we don't need to because Jesus, the only perfect sacrifice, has accomplished that once and for all). So, what did John mean when he instructed readers to lay down their lives? Thankfully John explained what he meant in the next few verses. In verses 17-18, we learn that to love our brother and sister manifests itself in our generosity and compassion. Showing compassion is the feeling; generously providing for their need is the truth in action. God calls His people to love in both word and deed. It is interesting that John switched from discussing the brothers and sisters (plural) to **a fellow believer** (singular) in verse 17. It is much easier to love an undefined need held by a large group of people (that won't require you to actually respond personally) than it is to get personally involved in helping a single brother or sister. Getting personally involved always requires more of us, and is a much better definition of what authentic love looks like.

LOVE LIKE JESUS

First John 3:16-18 defines what real love looks like: Jesus laid down his life for us. His willingness to go to the cross to die in our place shows us what love is.

We should also lay down our lives for our brothers and sisters. What might that look like in some real-world situations when ...

You see someone in obvious need as you travel to and from work?

You know someone in your community is struggling with the loss of a job?

You see parents struggling with their young children?

You witness anger in a teenager you know?

You hear an acquaintance seems to be struggling emotionally?

ILLUSTRATOR PHOTO/ BRENT BRUCE (91/B/0053)

Above: Beit Jimal Monastery south of Beit Shemesh. It is identified as the burial site of Gamaliel, Stephen, and Nicodemus. John might well have remembered Jesus' conversation with Nicodemus (John 3) as he described love in 1 John 3:16-18.

John remembered a conversation Jesus had about the love the Father has for us in that famous interaction at night with Nicodemus. He recorded that interaction in John 3.

It is much more difficult to meet the need of a person right in front of you than to profess your love for an anonymous group.

In verse 18, John gave what perhaps could be considered the central point of the letter. Christians are not called to talk a big game. They are not called to express their love only through their words; rather, they are called to put their love into action. This applies to the way we express our love toward God and the way we express our love toward others. John would continue to expound upon this truth later in the letter (chapter 4), but it is clearly a point of emphasis here as well. The reason John called believers to love in both word and deed is because this was the ministry of Jesus. People wanted to be around Jesus because He loved them. Jesus loved the sick (Matt. 14:14). Jesus loved the children (Luke 18:16). Jesus loved the hungry (Matt. 15:32). Jesus' entire ministry was based on displaying love in unexpected ways. In fact, His ultimate act of love was that He gave Himself as the propitiation for our sins. Jesus did not just talk about love, He revealed in His flesh the love of the Father toward us in that while we were yet sinners, Christ died for us (Rom. 5:8). Therefore, we must also love with our actions.

FEELINGS CAN BE DECEPTIVE (1 JOHN 3:19-24)

Lies. Everyone has told one, or two, or a thousand, over the course of their lives. Kids tell them; employees tell them; bosses tell them; coworkers tell them; boyfriends tell them; spouses tell them; and our enemy, Satan, is master of them. Everyone has told a few, because every one of us is a sinner. It has been said there are only two types of people in the world, sinners and repentant sinners. While it might be easy to think about certain people who tell lies, the reality is that one of the most dangerous exporters of falsehood is one's own feelings. One of the most frustrating experiences any pastor faces is the couple who has come to him for marriage counseling, when one of the partners is camping out on the idea that he or she "doesn't have any feelings" for the other person anymore. Somewhere along the way, the person bought into the lie that feelings are required to make a marriage work. Scripture warns us against trusting our feelings. Jeremiah said, "The heart is more deceitful than anything else, and incurable—who can understand it?" (Jer. 17:9). John also understood this truth, because in verses 19-20 he told readers that when their feelings lie about their salvation, when they have doubts about their faith, they can look to the way they love other people to verify the truth that is in them.

GOD AND LOVE

John's words to believers in 1 John 4:7-11 dig deeply into the heart of God's love and how it changes us. Use the following activity to review the truths taught in these powerful verses.

Fill in each blank with the word "God," "God's," or a form of "love" ("love," "loves," "loved").

Dear friends, let us _____ one another, because _____

is from _____, and everyone who _____ has been born

of _____ and knows _____. The one who does not

_____ does not know _____, because _____ is

_____. _____ _____ was revealed among us in this

way: _____ sent his one and only Son into the world so that

we might live through him. _____ consists in this: not that we

_____ _____, but that he _____ us and sent his Son

to be the atoning sacrifice for our sins. Dear friends, if _____

_____ us in this way, we also must _____ one another.

He assured them that while their feelings might deceive them, God will not be fooled. When we have those moments of doubt, we can always return to the truth of 1 John 1:9 and approach Him with a spirit of confession and repentance. When we confess our sins, we recalibrate our hearts to the fact that we are forgiven and cleansed. While we cannot rely on our emotions and feelings, we can rely on our Savior Jesus and on His Word. The final way God confirms our salvation is by sealing us with His indwelling Holy Spirit. Someone who is truly saved will confess personal sin, remain faithful to Jesus as the Messiah, love neighbors, and see the fruit of the Spirit produced in his or her life.

WHAT IS LOVE? (1 JOHN 4:7-11)

Many a preacher has attributed the statement "I take my text and make a beeline to the cross" to the great English preacher Charles Spurgeon. Though he apparently never made such a statement, it does poignantly stress that no matter what text or doctrine we are teaching or preaching, we need to help people see how that doctrine is tied directly to the cross. John did this faithfully. He had already made multiple references throughout his letter to how our love for others must be derived from what Jesus has done for us, but in chapter 4 he made it specifically clear. He began this section of his letter by repeating the idea that if we are not loving people well, then we do not know God. This time he specified why. The reason is that **God is love.** Love is part of the very nature of God Himself. When we come to faith, we are filled with the Spirit of God. This means that we have become the temple of God (1 Cor. 6:19-20). This means God's Spirit dwells in believers. This will cause a transformation of our hearts and lives. If God is love (and He is), then His transforming work in our lives through His Spirit will transform us into people who love. If we are not becoming more loving in word and deed, then it ought to raise a serious concern for us about our salvation (1 John 4:8). John expanded this idea by clearly articulating the message of the gospel. He started this progression with God. God is love and we are sinners. We do not have the capacity to love within ourselves. We can only love because we bear the image of a loving God, but what does love actually look like? Love is defined by God because it is from Him. He is the Creator and Originator of it, so He is the only One who can accurately define it. The creator is always the one who can apply a value to something. When my kids bring home "art" or "crafts" from church or school, they have ascribed a certain value to the work. While others may look at their projects and see some craft sticks and paint, my kids see a work of art that ought to be displayed in an art gallery. The reason children see something in their art projects others do not see is that they created it. There is a value placed on it the work others do not share. As parents, and ones who loves those children deeply, we find their craft-stick art amazing. We love it because we love them, and they have ascribed a high value to it. It is the same with our heavenly Father. We want to love what He loves because we love Him and He has ascribed a value to certain things. Our Creator is God, and He has placed infinite worth upon us and therefore He has lavished His love upon us. In fact, He loved us so much, as John said, that He "sent his Son to be the atoning sacrifice for our sins" (1 John 4:10).

REMAINING IN LOVE (1 JOHN 4:12-21)

No one has ever seen God. John wrote these words to correct the false teaching of the Gnostics. Many of them claimed to have had special revelation of God and to have made a journey into heaven itself. These visions or journeys, they claimed, had allowed them to see God. John emphatically identified these experiences as heresy. These type claims were not limited to John's readers in the first century. There has been a recent uptick in "heaven-tourism" stories where people have claimed to have died and visited heaven. We must be just as diligent in our ability to discern false teaching as John was about pointing it out. The fact is no one has seen God. So how do we believe in a God we have never seen? John had just given one basis in verses 7-11. We can believe in the Father because we have seen the Son. John unpacked this thoroughly in his Gospel (John 14:9). The second reason we can believe in a God we haven't seen is that God has sent His indwelling Spirit into our lives to transform our capacity to love God and others. Paul affirmed this by teaching that, "God's love has been poured out in our hearts through the Holy Spirit who was given to us" (Rom. 5:5). John reiterated this by using language he had heard Jesus Himself use. Immediately before Jesus went to the cross, He spent a great deal of time teaching His disciples about how to experience the power of God in their lives (John 15). One of the primary things He shared with them was that in order to produce gospel fruit in their lives they must remain or abide in Him. The production of this fruit would be an outward indicator of inward transformation. Without this inward transformation, one must question whether or not one has been saved. If we were to read John 15:1-17 in detail, we would see exactly how Jesus tied the transformative work of the Spirit in our lives to our outward display of love toward God and others. In fact, what John wrote in 1 John 4 sounds very much like what Jesus taught in John 15–16. John concluded this portion of his letter by continuing to drive home how important it is for Christ-followers to be loving. It is impossible to emulate our Savior in any meaningful way apart from having deep love for God and people.

A CLOSER LOOK

Cain's Offering Rejected

I n this section of our study we looked at 1 John 3:11-12, where John wrote, "For this is the message you have heard from the beginning: We should love one another, unlike Cain, who was of the evil one and murdered his brother. And why did he murder him? Because his deeds were evil, and his brother's were righteous." As mentioned earlier, John did not shed much light on why Abel's offering was accepted and Cain's was rejected by God. Thankfully, there is another passage of Scripture that may help us to see one of the reasons why God may not have accepted Cain's offering. That passage is found in Hebrews 11:4, but we need to see the context. Hebrews 11 is one of the most familiar passages in the Scripture. It is often called the Hall of Faith. The writer set up the chapter by defining faith as "the reality of what is hoped for, the proof of what is not seen" (Heb. 11:1). He then gave us an important clue about how we are to understand the faith of those he listed. He told us that it is by faith that "our ancestors were approved" (v. 2). Now, with that in mind, let's look at verse 4 which mentions Cain and Abel. Here is how it reads: "By faith Abel offered to God a better sacrifice than Cain did. By faith he was approved as a righteous man, because God approved his gifts, and even though he is dead, he still speaks through his faith." It has often been said that God accepted Abel's offering because it was a blood offering and rejected Cain's because it was produce of the field, but this offering happened before any laws regulating offerings. Also, there were grain offerings that were commended throughout the Old Testament (Lev. 2 and elsewhere), so if it was not the offering itself that brought rejection, then perhaps it was the way in which it was offered. The writer of Hebrews stated that it was faith that received God's approval. The fact Abel is mentioned as one whom God accepted seems to imply he offered his offering in faith and Cain did not. Had Cain approached God by faith, it seems God would have accepted his offering and extended His approval.

Personal Reflection

1. Have you ever experienced hatred from the world as a result of living out your faith? Explain. How did you respond?

2. Who is the hardest person in your life to love and why?

3. Describe a time in your life where your feelings told you something you knew was contrary to the Scripture. How did you respond? What does it take to live by what we know rather than by how we feel?

4. What are some tangible ways we can express our love toward God? Toward others?

LIVING AS CONQUERORS

1 JOHN 5:1-21

I t is a great time to be alive. I often sit back and think about some of the technology available to us now that really makes our lives so much easier. There is the mobile phone, the laptop computer, and digital music, just to name a few. However, one of my favorite pieces of technology is the digital video recorder (DVR) and the ability to digitally record live television events. This has changed the way I watch sports. Now I don't have to rush home on a Saturday to catch my favorite college football game.

Not long ago I was watching my team play when my wife informed me it was time to leave to meet another couple for dinner. At first, I was not thrilled about leaving the game in limbo, but I realized I was recording it, and therefore would be able to finish it when we returned home. On the way to dinner it just so happened the game was on the radio, so I decided to listen. The trip to the restaurant took just long enough for me to finish listening to the entire game. It was a very close game with my team pulling out the victory in the last minute. When we returned home after dinner, I turned the game on to watch what I had already listened to. The fact that I already knew my team won in the end made me want to watch the game even more.

Just like my DVR recorded the entirety of the football game so I could view the end, the Bible has recorded how human history will culminate in the return of Christ. It shows us how Christ and His kingdom are victorious. It reminds us that when we belong to Jesus, we are on the winning side. We are more than conquerors.

CONQUERING THROUGH OBEDIENCE (1 JOHN 5:1-4)

John liked definitive statements. We have seen several throughout this letter, and we see some more here in chapter 5. An atmosphere of confusion or fogginess requires leaders to speak with great clarity. Good leaders leave no room for doubt or confusion. John displayed his leadership by speaking into a situation where the Gnostics had confused the flock. The false teachers had sown seeds of doubt about who Jesus is, what sin is or is not, and how the people of God should treat each other. In order to quickly correct these false teachings, John spoke the truth boldly and clearly. He began this section of the letter by proclaiming the centrality of Jesus in salvation. Only those who believe **that Jesus is the Christ,** the Messiah, are born again. Those who love God also love His Son. You cannot love God and reject His Son. A parent or grandparent understands this reality on an earthly level. If people tell us they love us yet reject our family or do not show loving kindness toward them, those people do not really love us. Our families are extensions of us. People who truly love us will love our families. If this is true of earthly relationships, how much more so of God, especially since the Father and the Son share the same nature. If we do not love God's Son, then we do not love God. John spoke clearly against the false teaching of the day with this statement. He wanted his readers to fully embrace Jesus as the Messiah.

Once John explained how we know that we love the Father (i.e., by believing in His Son), he gave direction as to how we can know that we are loving people. So much of this letter was written to instruct believers to love each other that John needed to make sure the recipients understood exactly what that looked like. The answer he gave may come as a surprise. He did not say we should treat others the way we want to be treated. Instead, he said we love people by obeying God. Sometimes the most loving thing we can do in a person's life isn't what makes the person the most comfortable or what they would ask us to do. If we have children we must discipline them. They might conclude or claim we don't love them as a result, but the exact opposite is true. If we don't discipline them, then we are neglecting them, failing to show love. Letting sin go unaddressed is not loving. We live in a culture today that frequently says letting people do whatever they want is the way we show love toward them. But there is no truth in that. John wrote that holding up God's standards through obedience is the greatest way we can demonstrate love. He had already stated his basis for this, that God is love (4:8,16). Therefore, whatever He has commanded is the most loving action there is. To walk in full obedience to Him allows us to demonstrate the most authentic aspects of love to those we encounter.

John continued with this line of thinking by reminding his readers that following God's **commands are not a burden.** Following someone on the basis of a relationship, rather than rules, always eases the burden. This does not mean fleeing sinful passions is easy; rather, it means walking in obedience, while seeming costlier in the beginning, is actually less costly in the long run. There is an often used but on point preacher quote that says, "Sin will take you farther than you want to go, keep you longer than

 LOVING THE FATHER

First John 5:1-4 is loaded with precise descriptions of what it means to be a child of God. Did you read it carefully? Try to match the following questions with the correct answers below.

Questions
1. Who has been born of God? _____

2. What do we know about everyone who loves the Father? _____

3. How can we know that we love God's children? _____

4. Why aren't God's commands a burden? _____

5. What is the proof that we have conquered the world? _____

Answers
A) Everyone who has been born of God conquers the world.

B) We love God and obey His commands.

C) Everyone who believes that Jesus is the Christ.

D) Our faith gives us the victory over it.

E) They love the one born of Him.

Correct Responses: 1. C; 2. E; 3. B; 4. A; 5. D

you want to stay, and cost you more than you want to pay." This is so true. Sin is costly. You might not think so at first, but when the debt comes due (and it *always* comes due), it will be much more burdensome than resisting temptation and obeying the commands of God. John finished this thought with something encouraging. He reminded his readers of their position in Christ. This is good news for us as well. Just about the time we may be discouraged in our sin, God reminds us of **the victory.** The phrase John used, **conquers the world,** is a present active indicative in the Greek. This means that Jesus has already overcome the world (John 16:33), and if we remain in Him, we too are conquerors. We are victorious only because He is victorious. How then do we remain in Christ? The answer according to John is found in one thing, **our faith** in Jesus.

CONQUERING THROUGH FAITH (1 JOHN 5:5-13)

The apostle Paul said we are saved by faith alone, and this is true. But one important disclaimer to this truth is to ask in what or who we have placed this faith. The object of our faith determines the value of possessing faith. If we believed with one hundred percent faith that we were birds, and we went to the top of a tall building with one hundred percent faith we could fly if we jumped off the top, we would be painfully disappointed as we traveled quickly down to the earth below. We can possess all the faith in the world, but if it is placed in the wrong person or thing, it can be disastrous. John understood this and wanted to make sure his readers knew where to place their faith. Following his reminder about the victory that has been secured by faith, John focused his attention on the only One worthy of our faith, Jesus. We become conquers of sin when we place our faith in the One who won that victory on our behalf, Jesus. Apart from the work of Christ we would not be conquerors, but rather we would be dead in our sin (Eph. 2:5).

Scholars have provided a variety of interesting interpretations for verses 6-8. The phrase **the one who came** clearly refers to the incarnation, but following that the clarity gets a some bit cloudier. Debate begins when we ask what exactly **water and blood** mean. Anytime there is a question about what a Bible text means, it is important to remember what the context is. We need to go back and remember that 1 John was written in part because false teachers (Gnostics) were deceiving people about the person and nature of Jesus. Therefore, as we think through these verses, we must remember that John was likely trying to push back on some

Arch of Titus constructed by Emperor Domitian in AD 82 to commemorate the victories of his father, Vespasian, and brother Titus shortly after Titus's death. It stands at the foot of the Palatine hill on the Via Sacra in Rome.

ILLUSTRATOR PHOTO: BRENT BRUCE (83/8/0764)

ILLUSTRATOR PHOTO/ BRENT BRUCE (83/B/0782)

ILLUSTRATOR PHOTO/ BRENT BRUCE (83/B/0786)

Above: Details of inside of the Arch of Titus.
Top: A relief depicting triumphant Titus (in horse-drawn chariot) led by the goddess Roma. People of Rome and the Senate follow the chariot.
Bottom: Depiction of the victory procession with various spoils from Solomon's Temple after the Jewish War. John taught believers are to live as conquerors.

Following his reminder about the victory that has been secured by faith, John focused his attention on the only one worthy of our faith, Jesus. We become conquerors of sin when we place our faith in the One who won that victory on our behalf, Jesus.

of these false teachings. In this case it seems that **water** refers either to Jesus' physical birth (John 3) or to His baptism. The **blood** likely refers to His death on the cross. Much of the false teaching of the Gnostics revolved around denying the humanity of Jesus. John appeared to want to draw his readers back to these truths by mentioning Jesus' birth and death, both very physical events. The mention of the **Spirit ... who testifies** is to verify the truth of these claims. The Holy Spirit confirmed Jesus' physical birth (Luke 1:35) and baptism (3:22).

One of the functions of the Holy Spirit is to lead us into all truth (John 16:13). **Human testimony** is all well and good, but the testimony of God Himself is unbreakable. When we belong to Jesus, we not only have our own testimony, but we have the Holy Spirit who also testifies on our behalf (Rom. 8:16). To deny that Jesus is the Messiah, or that He is the Son of God, is to deny God. To drive home this point, John returned to one of his favorite words, **liar.** Anyone who denies this truth is claiming that God is a liar, which, of course, is ridiculous.

The testimony of God is the ultimate source of truth. Even though our culture is rapidly running away from the things of God, the Bible is still used in courtrooms and at the swearing in of many judges and politicians. At these ceremonies, the person being sworn in places a hand on the Bible and swears to tell the whole truth, or in the case of a politician, swears to uphold the Constitution. Symbolically, to swear by someone or something, one must place oneself under the authority of a greater person or object. To swear on the Bible is to declare that God is a greater source of power and truth than the individual is. However, in this instance, God gave His own testimony because there is no one who possess greater truth than He does. This is why when a covenant was reached throughout the Old Testament, the only name God could swear by to uphold His end of the covenant was His own name (Gen. 22:16; Isa. 45:23; Jer. 49:13; Heb. 6:13). So, when God gives His testimony about His Son, there is not a greater source of truth He can call on.

Once John established that the testimony of God is true, he began to unpack the truth of it, and it is a powerful and glorious one. The testimony is this: **God has given us eternal life, and this life is in his Son. The one who has the Son has life. The one who does not have the Son of God does not have life.** This is the beautiful truth of the gospel. John wanted to make sure after everything else was communicated that the simple beauty of the gospel was proclaimed. John did not want people to walk away from his letter questioning whether or not they had eternal life. He wanted them to have confidence, not confidence in themselves or in their works, but confidence in Jesus, who gives eternal life through faith alone.

CONQUERING THROUGH PRAYER (1 JOHN 5:14-17)

In the movie *Facing the Giants,* there is a scene where Brock, the captain of the football team, is talking about how much stronger their opponent is than their team. The coach senses his lack of confidence in his own ability and in the ability of his teammates. The coach sees something in Brock and in the team that they do not see in themselves. In order to help the team see this, and to help them develop confidence, the coach calls on Brock to perform the death crawl, an exercise where an athlete must crawl on hands and feet like a bear without letting the knees touch the ground. In addition to only using hands and feet, a teammate rides on the crawler's back, making the exercise much more difficult. The team had been doing this exercise for short distances, so Brock assumes the coach wants him to do another round of thirty yards. When he calls Brock forward, Coach places a blindfold over Brock's eyes and asks him to go fifty yards and to give his very best effort. A teammate climbs on Brock's back and Brock begins to crawl. The team begins to cheer them on thinking Brock might make it fifty yards. It is clear this is a taxing exercise, and the coach continues to push and push Brock as he crawls. As Brock continues to go farther and farther down the field, his teammates begin to stand in amazement. When Brock finally falls to his knees and removes his blindfold, he has not gone thirty yards or fifty yards. He has gone the entire one-hundred-yard length of the field. In that moment the coach gets down in Brock's face and reminds him that if he walks around defeated, so will the rest of his team. What a picture of instilling confidence in someone. When we are walking by faith, in the power of the Holy Spirit, there is nothing we cannot accomplish for the kingdom.

One of the ways God develops our **confidence** in Him is through answering our prayers. The writer of Hebrews told us to approach "the throne of grace with boldness" (Heb. 4:16). When we come before God with our requests and needs, we can come with boldness and confidence, not because we are worthy, but because we come through the broken body and shed blood of Jesus (10:20). Coming to God through His Son ought to encourage us as we pray. John expressed this confidence in his letter by reminding his readers that God **hears** our prayers when **we ask anything according to his will.** (We will examine what it means to pray according to

God's will in A Closer Look.) To have confidence and boldness, we must have a proper understanding of what prayer is and what it is not. The Holman New Testament Commentary explains how we ought to approach prayer; "Prayer must be viewed not as our attempt to get God to see things from our point of view but as our attempt to see things from God's point of view. When we grow, mature, study, and meditate on Scripture and seek the will of God, we try to ask ourselves not what *we* want, but what *God* wants."[1] John wanted his readers to be people of prayer, because knowing we have access to the power of God in prayer will allow us to walk as confident conquerors in this world.

In addition to praying for what we need, John directed his readers to pray for each other, especially those who might be struggling in sin. There is an interesting phrase that John used as part of his directive to pray. He said, **If anyone sees a fellow believer committing a sin that doesn't lead to death, he should ask, and God will give life to him.** Scholars have debated often over what type of sin this might be. There is no consensus on how to interpret this passage, and even the best explanations are not without controversy. Some scholars have suggested that it is apostasy, the denial of the faith by someone who once claimed to walk in it. This would seem to contradict John's earlier word when he declared that true believers cannot fall away (1 John 3:9). Another suggested explanation is that it refers to blaspheming the Holy Spirit. If this is the case, why would John call him **a fellow believer?** A third suggested explanation is that it refers to a sin that leads to physical death. Examples of this might be Ananias and Sapphira (Acts 5), the man who practiced sexual immorality with his step-mother (1 Cor. 5), or perhaps even those who died from taking the Lord's Supper in an unworthy manner (ch. 11). The problem with this view is that it would be impossible to know when it was too late to pray, and one would not know which sin it was that was leading to death until perhaps after the person had died. Therefore, because we cannot know exactly what the sin that leads to death is, we should focus our attention on the other side of the directive and commit ourselves to praying for our brothers and sisters who may be struggling with sin in their lives.

CONQUERING THROUGH TRUTH (1 JOHN 5:18-21)

As John concluded his letter, he circled back around to how Christians ought to act. What behaviors are to be reflected in the life of someone who is saved? The answer John landed on is the same as the one he began with.

WATCHFUL AND CAREFUL

The synopsis of John's warning in 1 John 5:18-21 could be our reminder to be "watchful and careful." We've been given the power to overcome sin, but evil is in our world.

Write at least one way you can be watchful and careful in each of the following situations:

At work

In your home

With close friends

Among strangers

In what you watch

At church

In traffic

With extended family

Those who belong to God do not make the practice of sin a part of their daily lives. Instead they pursue a holy life that seeks the favor and protection of God. This is important because we do have an enemy, **the evil one,** that seeks to destroy us. We must be watchful and careful as we walk in this world. As Warren Wiersbe said, "Christians do not keep themselves saved, but they do keep themselves out of the snares of the devil."[2] We can have confidence when we live according to the Spirit and not according to the flesh. Walking in the Spirit is what sets us apart from the world. While the enemy has sway and dominion over this world, believers are able to walk in the confidence of Christ. John concluded his letter with a bit of practical theology that, if practiced, will save a believer a lot of heartache and will help him or her follow the way of Christ. That command was to **guard yourselves from idols.** To be a conqueror we must resist the worship of anything or anyone but Christ.

A CLOSER LOOK

1 John 5:14

Shakespeare once wrote, "We, ignorant of ourselves, beg often our own harms, which the wise powers deny us for our good; so find we profit by losing of our prayers." In 1 John 5:14, John provided an important insight into our prayers. God always promises to hear the prayer of believers when they pray according to His will. This is certainly the pattern of New Testament teaching on prayer beginning with Jesus when he declared, "Your kingdom come. Your will be done on earth as it is in heaven" (Matt. 6:10). Praying according to God's will begins by having the right perspective on who God is and who we are. We exist to bring glory to God and to expand His kingdom (1 Cor. 10:31). God does not exist to provide for all our wants and comforts. Therefore, our prayer life should reflect this. We should not pray simply to promote our own agendas or to make our lives more self-focused (Jas. 4:3). Praying God's will means we must understand what is on the heart of God. We can do this by following the patterns of God's Word. For instance, we know we are to pray for people to be saved (Rom. 10:1). We are to pray for forgiveness when we sin (1 John 1:9). We are to pray for boldness to declare the gospel (Acts 4:29). We are to pray for those in authority over us (1 Tim. 2:1-2). These are just a few examples of how the Scripture can provide insight into God's will for our prayers. The amazing thing about prayer is that even when we do not know how to pray God's will, His Spirit will still help us by interceding on our behalf. Paul told us in Romans 8:26-27 that "the Spirit also helps us in our weakness, because we do not know what to pray for as we should, but the Spirit himself intercedes for us with inexpressible groanings. And he who searches our hearts knows the mind of the Spirit, because he intercedes for the saints according to the will of God." Therefore, we must pray. We must pray in faith, and we must pray with fervency. Knowing God's Word will help us pray God-sized prayers because our God "is able to do above and beyond all that we ask or think" (Eph. 3:20). Praise His glorious name!

Personal Reflection

1. What are some areas in your life where you feel least like a conqueror?

2. When have you loved someone in a way you knew pleased God, but perhaps the person did not see it that way? When has someone loved you in such a way, but you failed until later to recognize that love?

3. What have you previously put your faith in that did not deliver? When have you trusted God and He proved faithful?

4. What are some things God commands us to pray for that you feel confident about when you pray for them?

1. David Walls and Max Anders. *I & II Peter, I, II & III John, Jude*, Holman New Testament Commentary, Vol. 11. (Nashville: Broadman & Holman, 1999), 225.

2. Warren W. Wiersbe, *Wiersbe's Expository Outlines on the New Testament* (Wheaton, IL: Victor, 1992), 778.

FAITHFUL TO TRUTH

2 JOHN

INTRODUCTION AND GREETING (2 JOHN 1-3)

We live in a time of division in America. People seem to passionately disagree about almost everything. It has been difficult to find common ground on almost any significant issue facing our nation. We disagree about marriage, when life begins, gun ownership, race relations, immigration, borders, economics, and schools. There are a lot of contributing factors to this division, with social media at least contributing to some degree. There was once a time when people could hold an opinion without sharing it with the world. However, it now feels like we have to let our opinions be known about every issue from the weather, to politics, to sports, to what we ate for dinner. To make matters worse, not only do we feel the need to express our opinion on almost every subject, but we also feel the need to let other people know that they hold an opinion inferior to ours. These expressions are not taking place within the confines of relationships built on love and trust, but they are expressed loudly and broadly to the world. Sadly, this type of behavior has not been limited to the world. It has crept into the church and into the way professing believers treat other Christ-followers. Some of the worst posts on social media in the past few years have been between two people claiming to be Christians. While they might not have used "bad" language or posted inappropriate pictures, they attacked and accused each other. They undermined, belittled, and stirred divisive attitudes. The worst part of this is that they attempted to do it under the banner of "protecting the truth" or "discerning" what the true Christian position

Patmos, the place of John's exile and from which he wrote the Book of Revelation. As John encouraged "the elect lady and her children" (2 John 1) to be "Faithful to Truth," so he himself remained faithful in preaching the gospel even though it cost him his freedom.

ILLUSTRATOR PHOTO/ BOB SCHATZ (28/1/11)

ILLUSTRATOR PHOTO/ G.B. HOWELL/ BOSTON MUSEUM OF FINE ARTS (64/2076)

Left: Domitian was the Roman Emperor from AD 81 to 96. Historical sources from the Roman period portray him as a vicious tyrant. It is commonly believed Domitian was the emperor who exiled John to Patmos.

on every issue ought to be. Often times those "discerning" what is true and right seem to care very little about the people they intend to correct. They appear to be far more interested in being seen as right. Ironically, many times they seem to have lost sight of the truth in their attempt to be right. This leads to divisive teaching and unfaithful teaching. It also leads to a lack of love toward one another. John wrote to encourage his readers to stay focused on the truth, but to not stop loving other people. While they might not have been expressing all these ideas on social media, John knew that a true follower of Christ is motivated not only by the **truth,** but also by love.

John wrote his second letter in part to address what it means to walk in the truth while loving other people. To open this letter, John referred to himself as **the elder.** He also did this in 3 John. This was an interesting way to open a letter. It is also an interesting way to describe oneself. This introduction raises several question for us today. What was John trying to communicate by the choice of this title? Was John the lady's elder at her local church (he immediately addressed the letter to **the elect lady)?** We cannot be sure, but it is likely the term **elder** was to imply spiritual maturity and apostolic authority rather than to identify his role in this specific church or with this specific lady. The fact this letter was addressed to **the elect lady** leads to several other unanswered questions. Was this letter to an individual lady and her kids or to an entire church? Scholars are divided on this matter. We will leave that question open as it does not significantly impact how we examine the doctrinal distinctions. What we do know is that this letter is one of the shortest books in the New Testament, yet it is packed with truth. In the letter, John intended to encourage followers of Christ to seek the truth and to express authentic Christlike love toward others. It was important for John to teach them to stand for what was doctrinally sound, but to do so in an atmosphere of love and grace. One thing we will see as we study this letter is that John began with words like: **grace, mercy, peace, truth,** and **love.** He knew that for people to listen to his instruction, they must first understand that he loved them and was full of grace, mercy, and love toward them. This letter may only be 245 words in the Greek, but John used the word **truth** five times and the word **love** four times. While 2 John is a short letter, it is packed full of the truth and love we need to hear today.

WALKING THE TRUTH (2 JOHN 4-6)

Several people made a profound impact on my faith as I was growing up. One of these was my student minister. He came to our church as I was transitioning from our children's ministry into our student ministry (we called it *youth group* back then). Over the next several years, he would teach, lead, and love our group. He was called to serve another church when I was a junior in high school, and I was deeply saddened when he left. Several years later (after I had graduated from college), I was serving as a chaperone on a student ministry event in the church I was attending. The camp pastor spoke about how we ought to show honor to those who influenced our lives in significant ways. He suggested writing a letter to one of the people who had contributed to our strengthened faith. I decided to write my former student minister. In my letter I expressed my deep appreciation for how he had helped me grow, what God had done in my life since, and what He was doing at the moment. I sent the letter, and I never really thought about it again. A month or so later I checked my mail only to see I had a letter from him. I will never forget the opening line of his letter to me. His letter began, "Dear Chad, I am very glad to know that you are one of my children who is walking in the truth (2 John 4)." I have never forgotten that opening. It made a significant contribution to the way I pastor today. I want to lead those under my influence in such a way that many years from now they will still be **walking in truth.**

The truth is a strange thing. We say we want to know the truth. We believe we want to know the truth. But we are not always ready to hear or accept the truth. The fact is, God not only wants us to know the truth, He has provided a way through His Son Jesus for us to know it and walk in it. John wrote 2 John to express his gratitude and excitement that there were some who had not been fooled by the false teachers and were still very much remaining faithful to the truth they had been taught. Walking in the truth is the first step to walking with God. We cannot truly know God if we do not know Him as the truth. It should be no surprise Jesus said, "I am the way, the truth, and the life. No one comes to the Father except through me. If you know me, you will also know my Father. From now on you do know him and have seen him" (John 14:6-7). Knowing the Father means knowing the Son, and when we know the Son, we know the truth. Without knowing the truth about God our love will be misplaced. This is why John implied that we love on account of the truth, because we know the One who is both truth and grace (1:14). We cannot separate what we believe from how we behave.

Truth rightly applied through the gospel is applied in love. John reminded us of the commands of Jesus. What he was conveying was not something new. It was not **a new command,** but it was the command at the heart of Jesus' teaching. This would immediately set apart John's teaching from the Gnostics, who believed they had a new word from God. We should always be nervous and skeptical when people come to us and say they have a "word from the Lord." Any word from the Lord will be anchored in Scripture and will actually not be a "new word," but in fact it will be the words of the Scriptures brought to our heart or mind. God does not have a new word, He has given us His final word through His Son Jesus (Heb. 1:2). John again drew his readers minds back to the teaching of Jesus Himself in John 13:34, "I give you a new command: Love one another. Just as I have loved you, you are also to love one another. By this everyone will know that you are my disciples, if you love one another." John affirmed that what Jesus taught was sufficient, and there was nothing that needed to be added to it.

There are two primary ways we see the truth misrepresented or misappropriated. The first is when we see people attempt to add to it. Every year around Christmas and Easter, television networks run special "documentaries" claiming to have new information or evidence we should consider as we reflect on the birth or death of Jesus. Often these "documentaries" will talk about a "new gospel" that has recently been discovered. Each time these pseudo-documentaries air, they are attempting to undermine the truth of the Scripture by claiming there is more God wants to say to us that is not included in the Scripture. Just like John's readers who were being led astray, we also must guard our hearts and minds from being led astray by such myths and falsehoods.

The second way we see truth misapplied is when we hear people talk about love. Many of us regularly hear others talk about how we should love people and that Christians are more judgmental than they are loving.

We certainly know some Christians who are not as loving as they could be or ought to be. But most of the time when we hear people say this, what they mean is Christians are not accepting my sin and loving me like I am. When I counsel married couples going through difficult times, I too often hear one spouse say something along the lines of, "Well, he/she does not really make me happy anymore, and I know God wants me to be happy." My usual response is that God want you to love your spouse more than you love yourself, and therefore your happiness is second to your faithfulness.

WATCH YOURSELVES

John's second letter contains a stern warning: Many deceivers have gone out into the world and don't confess the coming of Jesus Christ in the flesh. He solemnly instructed recipients to "watch yourselves" (2 John 8).

What does it mean to "watch yourselves"?

Who or what sets the standard for how we should carefully walk?

How can others help you to keep an eye on yourself?

What personal standards have you set for your own journey of life?

In what areas are you most tempted to be deceived? Why is that?

This is usually not well received, as the person is usually hoping I will affirm the unhappiness and provide relief or a way out of the marriage. Eventually, what comes out of these meetings is the claim that I am not loving the person, because I don't care about his or her feelings. Of course, this is not true, but what is being implied is that to love someone we must sacrifice the truth. John actually said the opposite. If we are really going to be able to love people, it must be in the context of what is true. If we are afraid to walk in the truth, we can never actually love people the way Jesus did. Jesus always demonstrated grace and love, but He never affirmed people's sins. He always called them to repentance. Love and truth work together, and John desired for his readers to understand this. This is why John defined love as obedience: **This is love: that we walk according to his commands.** He reminded his readers they could not claim to love God without walking according to the truth.

STAY ALERT! (2 JOHN 7-11)

The crux of the letter is found in verses 7-8 as John revealed the reason for his letter. He wanted to warn readers about the false teaching surrounding the incarnation of Jesus. He warned readers to stay alert and be on the watch for those trying to lead them astray. In verse 7, he identified a specific false teaching to be alert for. Anyone who claims that Jesus, the Messiah, did not come bodily, or **in the flesh,** is a false teacher. Period. Not only was this false teaching prevalent among John's audience, it also appeared to be an issue for Paul in Corinth. In 1 Corinthians 15, Paul addressed an issue from a group of false teachers who were preaching no bodily (physical) resurrection. The reason both John and Paul had to address these false teachings is that the implications of this teaching has eternal significance for those who fall into its deception. In some cases, it might prevent someone from coming to faith in Christ; in other cases it could severely hinder our ability to know and walk with Him. For instance, Paul reminded those in Corinth that "if Christ has not been raised, your faith is worthless; you are still in your sins" (1 Cor. 15:17). If Jesus was not physically raised, then He did not defeat sin and death and we are still lost in our sins for eternity. The same can be said about John's case. If Jesus is not the Messiah in the flesh, then we are still sheep without a shepherd, and we are still under the law of death. These types of false teaching always originate from the devil. He has been deceiving with his crafty words since the garden of Eden when he asked Eve (Gen. 3:1), " 'Did God really say, "You can't eat from any tree in the garden"?' "

ILLUSTRATOR PHOTO/ DEBORAH CANTRELL (21/0473)

Anyone who claims that Jesus, the Messiah, did not come bodily, or in the flesh, is a false teacher. In 1 Corinthians 15, Paul addressed an issue from a group of false teachers who were preaching no bodily (physical) resurrection. The reason both John and Paul had to address these false teachings is that the implications of this teaching has eternal significance for those who fall into its deception.

Above: This memorial inside the Church of the Holy Sepulchre in Jerusalem houses the traditional site of Jesus' tomb. Another location within the church commemorates the place of Jesus' crucifixion. According to John 19:41-42, His tomb was close to the place of His crucifixion. The church was built to enclose both sites. The original church on this site was built and dedicated about AD 336 by Constantine the Great, the first Christian emperor.

Having addressed the danger on the outside (deceivers and false teacher), John next instructed his readers how to internally combat the deception. They were to stay alert and **watch** themselves. Staying alert means being constantly aware of what is coming in and out of one's life.

Our world is no different than the one John addressed. We have false teaching coming at us from multiple sources: television, social media, schools and so forth. A wise believer filters everything being heard and seen through the lens of the gospel. This filter allows the believer to stay aware of what is right and true. John urged his readers not to lose focus, not to get tired, but to stay alert and to **watch yourselves** carefully. If we can do this, then we will **receive** our **full reward.** But if we lose focus and fail to watch carefully, we will lose what we had spent so much effort to gain.

One thing I love to do is to run. I am not a fast runner, but I do enjoy the thrill of competing against my own times and my own body. I did not start running until about six years ago. Since then I have completed four marathons and fifteen half-marathons. One of the things I noticed not long after I started distance running was that my body took a long time to develop stamina and a short time to lose it. I would need to train for several months in order to run an entire half-marathon without stopping or walking, but I would only need to stop running for a few weeks in order to lose a lot of that endurance. One of my favorite races is the Indianapolis Monumental Marathon/Half-Marathon that happens in early November. I love this race because it is close to my home in Dayton, Ohio, and early November in the Midwest is a beautiful season for running. I have run this race (either the full or the half) three or four times. Each time I begin preparing during the summer months, and I train throughout the fall. I go to the race and usually do well (by my standards). I then go home and stop getting up early on Saturdays to train. I start eating more during Thanksgiving and Christmas. By the time January rolls around (less than two months later), I can barely run three miles. Somehow, I went from being able to run 26.2 miles in November to barely being able to run three miles seven weeks later.

Just like a runner losing his training stamina, a believer can lose the fruitfulness of the Christian life. John did not want the believers to miss their **full reward.** This teaching aligns closely to the words of Jesus in John 6:27-29 when He told His disciples: " 'Don't work for the food that perishes but for the food that lasts for eternal life, which the Son of Man will give you, because God the Father has set his seal of approval on him.' 'What can we do to perform the works of God?' they asked. Jesus replied, 'This is the work of God—that you believe in the one he has sent.' " The primary way our lives bear fruit is that we believe Jesus is the incarnate Messiah. When we believe that, it will should us to walk in love and

FACE TO FACE

In 2 John 12, John wrote:

"Though I have many things to write to you, I don't want to use paper and ink. Instead, I hope to come to you and talk face to face so that our joy may be complete."

How might you restate those sentences using twenty-first century technology and terminology?

Who in your life needs to hear the truth of love, joy, hope, or peace from you?

When and where can you make arrangements to speak truth to that person?

Who regularly speaks truth to your life, face to face?

How can you enhance your "real" relationships based on truth?

obedience to Him. If we fall for the false gospel of the deceivers and antichrists, we actually demonstrate that we do not really know God (2 John 9). An important aspect of belonging to Jesus is remaining in Him. Those who say they believe only for a short time then fall away actually demonstrate they never truly believed. They are like the seed that falls on the rocky places (Matt. 13:20-21). It may have looked like it had roots, but in the end it did not last and never produced fruit. Therefore, **Anyone who does not remain in Christ's teaching but goes beyond it does not have God. The one who remains in that teaching, this one has both the Father and the Son.** John concluded this section of his letter by warning his readers about the influences they allow to enter their lives. We should also be careful about whom we listen to, what we read, and what we watch. The evil one is crafty and a master of deception. We all know people we thought had sound doctrine but who in later years abandoned it for the lies of this world.

SIGNING OFF (2 JOHN 12-13)

This is the conclusion of John's second letter. His preference was to share these truths (and many others) with his readers in person, but he had not yet been able to **come to** them. The hard things are better said in person. There is too much emotion and love lost in written communication when oral communication is possible. John seemed to feel something similar. He would much rather have talked **face to face so that our joy may be complete.** John desired to come to them soon because of his deep love for them. When we love people, we want them to walk in the truth, we want them to be warned of the dangers, and we want to walk with them through it in person. John demonstrated here what the heart of an elder or pastor should look like.

A CLOSER LOOK

You or We?

One of the more interesting questions regarding 2 John is found in verse 8. Depending on what translation of the Scripture we read, we might see different wording. This is a result of something called textual variance. This simply means that some of the most reliable manuscripts use the phrase "what <u>you</u> have worked for" and some use "what <u>we</u> have worked for." If the correct reading is "you," it indicates that the reader should be careful to protect what their own faith has produced. If the proper reading is "we" (which I believe is the better of the two renderings), then it implies something huge that we should notice. Using the pronoun "we" implies that our faith is shaped by community—that others have poured into us and that the church, believing parents, and other followers of Christ have helped shape our faith. John seemed to indicate that he did not want his readers to lose what he (and others) had worked so hard to encourage and develop. In the opening verses of this letter, we saw how excited John was to hear that many of his recipients were still "walking in truth." Why would he be glad about this? He would be glad about it first because he loved Jesus and wanted people to know Him. But second, he would be glad because he had given his entire life's work to invest in these people. He was glad to hear that many had not lost what "we have worked for."

Personal Reflection

1. How does your life reflect that you are "walking in truth"?

2. After worship one day, a young man with whom you have struck up a relationship says, "I don't worry about all the doctrine stuff. I just believe in loving everybody." How do you explain to him the connection between doctrine/truth and genuine love?

3. What "deceivers" do you see at work in and around you? More importantly, how can you and other believers "watch yourselves" in such a way as to avoid being caught in the traps of the deceivers?

4. What are you doing to assure that you are "one who remains in" the truth of "Christ's teaching"?

HOSPITABLE IN TRUTH

3 JOHN

A TALE OF TWO CHURCH MEMBERS (3 JOHN 1-4)

I have often wondered how a church that has some of the most wonderful, kind, and godly people in it could also have some of the meanest, self-centered, and divisive people in it as well. John's third letter shows us that this is not a new phenomenon, but rather has been the case since the birth of the church. In this letter, the apostle John named three influencial men in the church. While these were actual men in the church at that time, we can see people with similar qualities in the church today. For a church to thrive, its members must pursue two of these types and lessen the impact of the other.

The first man was named **Gaius.** Gaius was a godly man who was faithfully **walking in truth** and practiced biblical hospitality to those who were taking the gospel to new places. The second man was named Diotrephes. Diotrephes was prideful and full of himself. He did not respect authority and instead spoke evil of the godly people in the church. He tried to control and manipulate the believers by removing them from the church as they attempted to display hospitality. The third man named was Demetrius. Demetrius was another godly man who practiced faith with integrity and faithfulness. As we look at what it means to walk in the truth and show biblical hospitality, we can learn from each of these men. In the cases of Gaius and Demetrius, we will see what we should do as we seek to practice hospitality and serve our churches in truth and grace. In Diotrephes we will see the person who is disruptive and does not seek to unite the church through hospitality, but instead works counter to the mission of the church. John's purpose for writing this letter was to call the followers of Christ to imitate what is good and to reject what is evil. This is also a strong word for us today.

John the apostle utilized a typical-of-the-time introduction in his third letter. He continued to refer to himself as **the elder.** John again wanted to establish his position of spiritual authority in this welcome, then address the intended recipient, Gaius. We immediately see that John was fond of his friend. Much of the letter was written to encourage and affirm the positive attributes of Gaius. One of the things we learn about Gaius in this introduction is that he was a **dear friend** of the apostle. I am not sure how life treated pastors (or even more so apostles) in that day, but every pastor (and every person) needs good friends. We need godly people outside our family who can help us share the burden of ministry. We need people we can be honest with about our hurts, fears, and joys. God did not create any of us to live in isolation. He gave Adam a wife in Eve, and He gave King David a friend in Jonathan. Paul was blessed by deep friendships with Silas, Timothy, and Titus. Scripture is full of examples of godly relationships. It appears John had one of these relationships with Gaius, and he wrote to praise his friend for continuing to walk in the truth. One other quick note on this friendship is that much like us with our friends, John genuinely appeared interested in all aspects of Gaius's life. He noted his prayer that Gaius was **prospering in every way and are in good health.** We do not know if Gaius had recently suffered through an illness or if John was simply stating this desire for Gaius. Too often we build friendships on what the other person can do for us. As soon as a relationship no longer benefits our immediate needs, we easily discard it and move to others who can meet those emotional or professional needs. We see here that John was not only concerned about Gaius's spiritual walk **(to the truth),** but he was interested in all of Gaius's life. We see this same truth reaffirmed at the end of the letter when John concluded by expressing his desire to see Gaius "soon" and "face to face" (v. 14).

As we saw in 2 John, the apostle rejoiced to hear that those he was close to continued **walking in truth.** John knew this not because Gaius told him, but because **fellow believers** had shared testimony with John about Gaius. As kids, when most of us got home from school, our parents may have asked us about our day. We most likely told them a few things and went on with our afternoon activities, leading our parents to assume all was good. However, on those days when one of our teachers sent home a note, those conversations usually changed, especially if the teacher's note told of us obeying, excelling on an assignment, or displaying kindness to another student. Talk about impressing our parents! I'm sure John felt the same way about Gaius. He was thrilled other people had noticed the exemplary life of Gaius as he walked faithfully in truth.

PARTNERING TOGETHER FOR THE SPREAD OF THE GOSPEL (3 JOHN 5-8)

During World War II, Hitler's Germany was killing Jews. This has become known to us as the Holocaust. Amidst that awful time there were those like Corrie ten Boom who were actively trying to save Jews from the hands of the Third Reich. Corrie ten Boom's father ran a watch shop on the first floor of their home. When the Nazi's invaded the Netherlands where the ten Booms lived, they built a secret room in the house. The ten Boom family would regularly hide Jews in their home in order to protect them from the Nazis. Eventually, the use of their home to protect Jews was discovered, and the ten Booms were arrested and sent to concentration camps. Corrie and her family put their lives in jeopardy in order to take in and protect strangers. It is well noted that one of the reasons they felt compelled to show this type of compassion and hospitality was their Christian faith. Receiving strangers, especially when it puts our own interests in danger, is an act of love that is noteworthy. In this letter, John commended Gaius for his own display of hospitality. In the case of Gaius, the **strangers** he took in were missionaries who were traveling across Asia Minor to spread the gospel of Christ. John referred to this action as a display of Gaius's faithfulness.

Hospitality was a very important aspect of life at that time. It was not uncommon to host people who were traveling. It was also not uncommon for those traveling while doing the work of the ministry to carry with them commendation letters from their home church to verify their purpose. We see examples of these letters when we look at the way Paul endorsed the work of Phoebe in Romans 16:1-2. There he wrote, "I commend to you our sister Phoebe, who is a servant of the church in Cenchreae. So you should welcome her in the Lord in a manner worthy of the saints and assist her in whatever matter she may require your help." Another example of this is in 2 John when the apostle warned the elect lady not to host anyone in her home who was actively spreading false teaching (2 John 10). Hospitality was an extremely important aspect of what it meant to be a believer in the first century. As a result of our changing culture, we do not always see the role of taking in strangers and providing for them in the same way as those in the early church.

On Memorial Day 2019, Dayton, Ohio, was struck by eighteen tornadoes in the matter of a few hours. The devastation was massive and widespread. Our church was notified and activated as an Emergency Red Cross shelter. Over the next two weeks we were the temporary home for dozens of families who had lost theirs in the storms. The way the people in our church and community stepped up to receive these families was so encouraging. People sacrificed their time and brought countless cases of bottled water to share with those in need because the water had been cut off to most of the city. Many people inviting others into their homes for baths and for meals. The response of the people reminded me of Gaius. These were not super Christians. They were not a bunch of pastors and deacons. These were ordinary people who loved Jesus and His church. We know nothing else about Gaius other than what John wrote here, but we can easily see how he acted faithfully in love and in truth toward those in need of hospitality.

As much joy as it is to extend hospitality, it can be a joy to receive it as well. When I graduated from college, I went on a mission trip to Namibia. The purpose of the trip was to prayer walk the entire country. For about nine days we drove all over the country. We prayed, we visited churches, and we shared the gospel. At every stop we stayed in a different church member's home. As a young man who had never been out of the United States, this was a comfort-zone-stretching experience. At our first stop I was pretty nervous about staying in a strange place with strange people, but by the end of the trip I had come to love the opportunity to meet, eat, and fellowship with these amazing people. While we may not have had much in common as the world sees it, we bonded quickly through our common faith in the Lord Jesus. The opportunity to receive their hospitality was an unforgettable blessing. As Christians, we have many opportunities to provide hospitality. In fact, one of the greatest opportunities we have to share the gospel with our neighbors is by inviting them into our homes for dinner and fellowship. There are far too many of us who cannot even name the people who live on our street. Imagine what God could do if we were intentional about fostering relationships with these neighbors by inviting them into our homes for a meal.

The Southern Baptist Convention has missionaries across the world. In order to fund those missionaries, we have a unified program of giving called the Cooperative Program. The CP, as it is often referred to, allows churches of all sizes to contribute together so that we can do together more than any one church could do alone. It is a brilliant plan for sending missionaries and supporting theological education. While it might be possible for my church to support one or two missionary families on the field, we could never provide all the training and resources that the International Mission Board is capable of providing. Therefore, we would be extremely limited in our ability as a church to really see much headway in our Acts 1:8 mandate. The great news is that John told the church that when they showed hospitality and **support** to those God had called to take the gospel throughout the world, they were in reality actively participating in the spread of the gospel itself. Even though Gaius was not the one traveling around the globe sharing the gospel and planting churches, his contribution to those who were made him an active participant in the work.

Church of St John at Ephesus commemorates the apostle's work in that city and is the traditional site of his tomb.

ILLUSTRATOR PHOTO/ TOM HOOKE (66/5/08)

When we give, pray, and support missionaries, we can be considered **co-workers with the truth.**

THE TROUBLEMAKERS (3 JOHN 9-12)

Most of us are aware of churches that are either plateaued or in decline. There are countless reasons why churches stop growing then decline. However, one reason churches struggle is when an ungodly person or group of people become the primary influences in the church. While we don't know the growth patterns of the church John was addressing, we do know that this type of troublemaker had emerged in a position of influence, and John intended to call him out. This man's name was **Diotrephes.** While we don't know much else about Diotrephes, what we do know about him is not flattering. John described him as someone who loved his own popularity. He loved the recognition that came with being a "leader" in the church. The problem is that every leader needs accountability and authority in life, and Diotrephes apparently disregarded and ignored the authority God had placed in his life through the apostle John.

As members of a local church, we need to be very careful how we speak of those God has placed over us. The writer of Hebrews warns us to "Obey your leaders and submit to them, since they keep watch over your souls as those who will give an account, so that they can do this with joy and not with grief, for that would be unprofitable for you" (Heb. 13:17). Diotrephes would have been wise to follow this truth, but instead he was busy slandering those in leadership with malicious words. We learn that Diotrephes was not only saying false and ugly things about John, but he also was failing to show hospitality to fellow believers. What made this behavior even worse was that he was expelling people from the church who were showing biblical hospitality. Sometimes it is people in the church who act in the most unbiblical ways. The great preacher Warren Weirsbe said that it is the action of church members like Diotrephes "that destroys churches. Eager for power and authority, they trample on the truth, ignore the Bible, grieve the Spirit, and scatter the flock."[1] Thankfully John would not stand for that.

Good leaders stand up to bullies. Pastors sometimes receive calls from a fellow pastor upset and thinking about resigning his pastorate. The disillusioned pastor often describes a group of individuals in his church who were spreading untruths about him or his family, undermining his leadership, and creating divisions within the church, thus destroying the church from the inside. Such behavior negatively impacts the church's ability to fulfill the Great Commission. Those pastors wind up spending all their time putting out the fires the disgruntled people start. Sometimes pastors in such situations feel as if there is not much they can do to correct the situation or defend the church from the ravages of such dissention. What a sad predicament. A shepherd must protect the flock. In John 10, Jesus described Himself as the Good Shepherd. In that text, He indicated that a shepherd protects his sheep. He does not leave them when the wolves

 DEAR FRIEND

Social interactions may be common, but dear friendships are not. Four times in 3 John, John referred to his "dear friend." Each "dear friend" is a blessing from God, and as stewards of His blessings we are to cultivate those friendships.

Who do you consider to be a dear friend? Why?

How do you invest in dear friend relationships?

How do you communicate with your dear friends? How often?

What encouragement can you give to a dear friend in the coming week?

How can your dear friendships inspire you to seek Jesus even more fully?

come, but rather he is willing to stay, fight, and even die for the sheep. While no pastor is Jesus, pastors must be willing to confront the wolves among the sheep. A good pastor protects the church from those (even within) who would devour the sheep. John put this teaching to good use in 3 John by his willingness to identify and confront Diotrephes.

After John identified the problem of Diotrephes, he urged Gaius (and the rest of the church) not to be like him. He described Diotrephes' words and deeds as **evil,** and he encouraged Gaius to do the opposite by practicing **what is good** and right. John then returned to one of his favorite themes: that our words and conduct tell the world about our relationship with God. When we do what is right and good, we indicate that we know and love God. When we practice evil and love the world and its ways, we indicate we do not know and walk with God.

Thankfully Gaius was not the only godly servant of the church. John mentioned another named **Demetrius,** who like John loved the truth and was walking faithfully in it. Demetrius had integrity that could be measured by the truth and observed by others in the church. Leaders in the church must exude both a propensity for truth and unwavering character. There is a reason Paul listed a life "above reproach" as a prerequisite for serving as an overseer in 1 Timothy 3:2. The church then needed men like Gaius and Demetrius, and the church today also needs men and women who love the Scripture and walk with impeccable character.

John closed his letter to Gaius by expressing his desire to come and see him in person, but for the moment this letter would have to suffice. He offered a traditional blessing of peace and asked Gaius to greet the other believers on his behalf. Verses like these easily can be read over due to their simplicity, but there are some important truths we ought to consider as we read them in our modern context. The first is that John valued relationships. He wrote to his friend and desired to see him in person. We live in a day of modern communication where it has never been easier to send text messages or emails. In addition, we can jump on our phones or computers and video chat with friends and family. This amazing technology will never replace being able to see someone in person and hug them, but believers ought to intentionally use these tools to connect with others. Hospitality is based on love, and love flows best through relationships. If we are going to walk in the truth and practice hospitality to others, we must prioritize relationships the way John did.

PRACTICE HOSPITALITY

John was not the only apostle of Jesus to write about hospitality. Peter instructed believers to "be hospitable to one another without complaining" (1 Pet. 4:9). Apparently, Peter had witnessed firsthand the frustration that sometimes comes with hospitality!

Practicing hospitality can be defined as welcoming the outsider in and treating that person like an insider. How are you practicing the skill of hospitality ...

In your home?

In your church?

In your community?

With acquaintances? Strangers?

To those traveling or needing a temporary shelter?

How are you inspiring others to be hospitable?

Whose hospitality inspires you?

ILLUSTRATOR PHOTO/ DAVID ROGERS (4/11/2)

Above: A building erected by King Herod over the caves of Machpelah at Hebron. Abraham bought the caves as a burial place for his wife, Sarah (Gen. 23). It was in this area that Abraham expressed hospitality to the three visitors of Genesis 18.

God's people were expected to demonstrate hospitality to others. An Old Testament example is Abraham welcoming the three visitors in Genesis 18.

A CLOSER LOOK

Biblical Hospitality

T he Greek word translated "support" in 3 John 8 literally means "to receive of" or "to take under." We can easily see the concept of receiving the hospitality of another or taking one under one's own roof or responsibility in an extension of hospitality. Indeed, the word is sometimes translated as "hospitality" (3 John 8, NIV). It implies that the favor being shown will be to those outside one's normal circle of friends and family. Biblical hospitality included food, shelter, and protection. God's people were expected to demonstrate hospitality to others. Some of the examples of this we see in the Old Testament Scripture are: Abraham welcoming the three visitors in Genesis 18, Laban receiving Abraham's servant in Genesis 24, Manoah's reception of the angel in Judges 13, and the reception Elisha received from the Shunammite family in 2 Kings 4. In the New Testament we see the concept with the sending out of the disciples in Luke 10 (perhaps this is where the apostle John learned the value of showing hospitality to traveling missionaries). We also see the practice affirmed in places like Hebrews 13:2 and 1 Peter 4:9.

The passage in 1 Peter directs believers to practice hospitality. This means we must be people who welcome the outsider and treat the person like an insider. This is certainly important in our individual lives and homes, but it is also vital we learn to practice this corporately in our churches. Unfriendly churches are not practicing hospitality any more than a Christian who turns away a missionary in need of respite.

Personal Reflection

1. Who are you more like, Gaius or Diotrephes? Would your pastor agree? Your lost neighbor?

2. Do you consider yourself someone who actively practices biblical hospitality? If so, how?

3. When have you been on the receiving end of hospitality? What do you think a biblical response to receiving hospitality ought to look like?

4. What can you personally do (not a church program, but you as an individual) to make your church or Bible study group more hospitable?

5. How can you help your pastor or church leaders deal with people like Diotrephes?

1. Warren W. Wiersbe, *Wiersbe's Expository Outlines on the New Testament* (Wheaton, IL: Victor, 1992), 783.